P9-AFA-841

DATE DUE

DEMCO 38-296

Involving Latino Families in Schools

To Dudley, my husband and co-creator
in the magic of relationship—

UNM-GALLUP   DUP

3 7996 1005 8243 2

Involving Latino Families in Schools

Raising Student Achievement Through Home-School Partnerships

Concha Delgado Gaitan

CORWIN PRESS
A Sage Publications Company
Thousand Oaks, California

Copyright © 2004 by Corwin Press.

All rights reserved. When forms and sample documents are included, their use is authorized only by educators, local school sites, and/or noncommercial entities who have purchased the book. Except for that usage, no part of this book may be reproduced or utilized in any form or by any means, electronic or mechanical, including photocopying, recording, or by any information storage and retrieval system, without permission in writing from the publisher.

For information:

Corwin Press
A Sage Publications Company
2455 Teller Road
Thousand Oaks, California 91320
www.corwinpress.com

Sage Publications Ltd.
1 Oliver's Yard
55 City Road
London EC1Y 1SP
United Kingdom

Sage Publications India Pvt. Ltd.
B-42, Panchsheel Enclave
Post Box 4109
New Delhi 110 017 India

Printed in the United States of America

Library of Congress Cataloging-in-Publication Data

Delgado-Gaitan, Concha.
Involving Latino families in schools: Raising student achievement through home-school partnerships/Concha Delgado Gaitan.
    p. cm.
Includes bibliographical references and index.
ISBN 0–7619–3137–6 (Cloth)—ISBN 0–7619–3138–4 (Paper)
   1. Hispanic Americans—Education. 2. Home and school—United States.
3. Education—Parent participation—United States. 4. Academic achievement—United States. I. Title. LC2670.D45 2004 371.829′68073—dc22

                                        2003026129

04   05   06   07   10   9   8   7   6   5   4   3   2   1

Acquisitions Editor:	Rachel Livsey
Editorial Assistant:	Phyllis Cappello
Production Editor:	Melanie Birdsall
Copy Editor:	Jacqueline Tasch
Typesetter:	C&M Digitals (P) Ltd.
Proofreader:	Teresa Herlinger
Cover Designer:	Michael Dubowe

Contents

Preface   vii

About the Author   xvii

1. **Life in Latino Families**   **1**
   Connecting   4
   Sharing Information   8
   Across Generations of Latinos   11
   Staying Involved   12
   Summary   14

2. **Connecting Latino Parents to the Classroom**   **15**
   Understanding Parent Involvement   19

3. **Sharing Information With Latino Parents**   **23**
   Connecting   24
   Informal Verbal Contacts With Parents   27
   Sharing Information   29
   Visiting Families   31
   Focus Groups   32
   Written Correspondence   32
   Language at Meetings   32
   Staying Involved   36
   Summary   39

4. **Instructing Parents to Teach at Home**   **41**
   Connecting   42
   Sharing Information   51
   Staying Involved   55
   Mentoring Project   58
   Summary   60

5. **Involving Families in the Life of the School**   **61**
   Connecting   62
   Sharing Information   64
   Parents as Advocates   66
   Home Experiences in the Classroom   69
   Parent Volunteers in the School   72
   Staying Involved   74
   Summary   81

6. **Preparing Latino Students for Higher Education**   **82**
   Connecting   83
   Sharing Information   87
   Summary   95

7. **Designing Schoolwide Parent Involvement Programs**   **97**
   Connecting   98
   Sharing Information   99
   Staying Involved   103
   Summary   110

8. **Forming School-Family-Community Partnerships**   **112**
   National Networking for Assisting Local Schools   113
   Grassroots Organizing for Latino Parent Involvement   117
   College Track Community Program   126
   Summary   130

Educational and Cultural Informational and
   Support Resources   **133**

References   **137**

Index   **141**

Preface

As Latino parents we have to help our children in every way possible. Simply because we don't speak English very well doesn't mean that we can't support our children to succeed in school. We value education, and there is much that we do at home every day. And staying involved in the school to watch over them is an extension of our parental responsibility.

[Translated from Spanish]

Addressing other Latino parents at a community meeting, this parent illustrates how Latino parents are willing partners in their children's schooling from preschool to high school. That parent involvement in children's schooling is both necessary and beneficial is beyond dispute. Parent involvement in students' elementary and secondary schooling has been a focus of much research over the past decades. Educators, including teachers, teacher assistants, community liaisons, counselors, principals, and other personnel, sometimes believe that because parents have less formal education or reside in lower socioeconomic communities, they are uncaring about their children's education. But research tells us that Latino parents do care about their children's education. Educators successfully include Latino communities in building strong partnerships on behalf of children.

National policies have identified parent involvement as a critical component of public education in the United States. The America 2000 national mandate for education promoted parent involvement: "Every school will promote partnership that will increase parental involvement and participation in promoting the social, emotional, and academic growth of children" (U.S. Department of Education, 2002, p. 1). As restated in the "No Child Left Behind Act," this decrees that parents should have a central role in their children's academic progress. They have the right to move their children out of persistently failing schools. To support parent involvement initiatives, Title I federal funds have been identified for schools that make parent involvement a priority, "with particular attention to parents who are economically disadvantaged, are disabled, have limited English proficiency, have limited literacy, or are of any racial or ethnic minority background" (U.S. Department of Education, 2002).

This book presents two key perspectives: (a) that parent involvement is an imperative component in the schooling of all Latino students and (b) that it is possible for educators and parents to collaborate in support of Latino students' academic success from the first day of their schooling career to the day they receive their high school diploma. That parent involvement is critical to school performance is beyond question. There is considerable evidence that parent involvement leads to improvement in student achievement, better school attendance, and reduced dropout rates (Becher, 1984; Epstein, 1987, 2001). Regardless of cultural and linguistic background, parents and schools can work together for the benefit of students.

The suggested activities, case examples, vignettes, ideas, and reflections found here are based on existing school and community efforts. The purpose of the book, however, is not to serve as a recipe book for educators to copy or to borrow ideas that have worked for others. Instead, this handbook offers discussions and suggestions for involving Latino parents who have been marginalized as a result of poverty, social and linguistic isolation, prejudice, or limited schooling. Educators can use these understandings as springboards for their own local reflection, planning, and designing of parent involvement activities and programs. Fundamentally, each school district and community must define its respective needs, resources, and goals to best serve Latinos in its particular setting. What is highly successful in one community may not fit the needs in another one because the trained personnel, fiscal resources, and student needs could differ enormously. However, as communities look within to identify their strengths, they can maximize schooling opportunities for Latinos. It is important to note that when schools complain about Latinos not being involved in their children's education, they are referring primarily to Latino parents whose experience with the schools has been deficient. These Latino parents may not have had any schooling in the United States, or they may have dropped out of school because they had difficult or negative academic and social experiences. When such people become parents, they may end up in low-wage employment with long hours. They may be unskilled in academics and unable to assist their children, or they may not speak the language of the school.

Furthermore, they may have difficulty accessing school resources to assist their children because they have little knowledge of how the school system works. In such cases, getting Latino parents involved in the school becomes problematic for educators. Involving parents who are strangers to the schooling system is possible if schools shape the conditions that invite open communication between Latino families and the school. Equity and access are the goals of parent-educator relationships. These two words represent the outcomes of all parent involvement efforts at the elementary and secondary levels because the fundamental purpose of all parent involvement is student achievement and academic success. Equity happens when Latino parents are participating in the schools on a par with their white Euro-American counterparts. This means that schools need to reach out differently to Latino parents and do whatever it takes to make them partners in the pursuit of Latino student achievement. Equity happens when the gap closes between white and Latino parent involvement and between white and Latino student achievement. Access is the process whereby Latino parents are able to attain information, resources, and entry into the schools to participate actively. That active level of participation enables community empowerment, where parents take charge of their schools, and it supports student achievement and success in school.

Life in Latino families is an important factor in the parents' level of participation in the school. The Latino family's home environment is affected by the family's socioeconomic standing, which could be serious economic poverty. By this, I do not mean that children from families who have low incomes cannot learn or that they necessarily have to underachieve in school. But we cannot ignore the fact that when children live in impoverished conditions, their resources differ from those available to families with higher incomes. Resources play a role in the education of the children. Although parents from poor communities value education for their children, they often lack knowledge about the educational system and the proper resources to effectively support their children's schooling. For example, poverty creates stress in the family due to financial insecurity. The lack of resources also results in health problems caused by poor nutrition and inferior or nonexistent health care, which in turn can negatively impact children's school attendance. In extreme cases, inadequate housing and homelessness interfere with children's schooling and learning because of frequent moving from place to place or not having the space to make schoolwork a priority at home (Lopez, 2002). These are not convenient excuses to link poor children with poor achievement, but social conditions can defeat children's motivation and opportunity to learn.

The issue of parent involvement raises issues beyond the practical strategies for involving parents in the school. From my own and others' more recent research, it is known that high-achieving Latino students report a high level of parent involvement at home and in the school (Delgado-Gaitan, 2001). These studies provide an understanding of the sociocultural complexity of the subject.

Educators need to establish a working partnership with Latino parents who live in poverty. The most important thing that educators can understand about Latino children from low-income homes is that they, too, have dreams. Families and children often overcome poverty and achieve success against the odds. Educators' attitudes about Latino children who are poor need to take into account that parents expect their children to receive a good education. Poor Latino children deserve to have educators believe in their intelligence and ability to learn. High expectations are critical for these children. Often, parents receive only negative reports about children from impoverished homes. Educators need to communicate with the parents about their children's strengths and efforts in school.

Studies of schools and Latino home culture have not always interpreted parental involvement in their children's schooling correctly. Although the use of English may be limited in many Latino homes, and parents may have low educational attainment, parents value education highly. They support their children's schooling by providing a strong emotional environment in the home. Telling children stories about family and personal history motivates them in their schoolwork and encourages them to take advantage of economic opportunities as adults. Many Spanish-speaking parents have immigrated to the United States, leaving behind family and facing tremendous peril to create opportunities for their children. This alone is a strong testament to Latino parents' desire to improve their children's future through education. A rift occurs when the school requires parents to play a role that is unfamiliar to them.

In educational institutions, parent involvement is based on knowing the needs of the children and the support system that is necessary for them to succeed. When students are not high achievers, educators often point the finger at the parents, if the parents are not visibly involved in the school. However, the relationship between families, communities, and schools is not a straight line linking parent involvement and grades on a student's report card. More important is the fact that learning is a lifelong process, and grades have to be understood in that specific context, underscored by the larger story of the complex Latino parental role in children's education. Simplistic parent involvement blueprints also minimize the students' learning process, as well as the teacher's role. This intricate relationship, negotiated day-by-day, impacts continuities and discontinuities back and forth from home to school to community.

Good home-school communication makes the job easier for the teacher and benefits students. If parents work closely with teachers, they will know the teacher's expectations, and the students will know that the parents and teachers are working together with consistency. Teachers note that communication between parents and teachers is the essence of Latino parent involvement. Weekly letters, frequent phone calls, positive notes to the parents, working with parent volunteers in the classroom, and educating parents in workshops are just a few ways that teachers ensure ongoing contact with parents. Some teachers believe that parent involvement is so important that they give parents their home telephone number. They receive calls until a fixed hour, such as 8:30 P.M.

Although teachers are aware of their responsibility to encourage parent involvement, they feel that the administration must support their efforts through district policies and activities that endorse student achievement. School districts assist teachers through release time, community liaisons, and training to help them to assist parents participate fully in their children's education.

Although there are many ways to accomplish parent involvement goals in Latino communities, three major conditions and objectives stand out. They are *connecting, sharing information,* and *staying involved.*

Connecting with Latino parents sends a strong message. When educators, whether teachers, teacher assistants, community liaisons, counselors, principals, or other personnel, reach out to parents in a language they understand, parents feel included in their children's education. When parents are intimidated by the school setting because of their inexperience, it matters even more that educators initiate contact to enlist parental participation in school programs.

Sharing information is a two-way process. Just as educators need to share with parents what is happening in the school, they also need to learn about the child's experience in the family.

Elementary and Secondary

POINT

Imperative Conditions for Latino Parent Involvement

- Connecting is . . .

  Reaching out to Latino families and community without judgment, in the language and culture that they understand, to keep information flowing

- Sharing information is . . .

  Improving learning opportunities for students through critical knowledge and sharing information between parents and educators about students

- Staying involved is . . .

  Involving Latino parents in an ongoing process by continuously assessing and revising the parent involvement program

Since parent involvement is an ongoing process, *staying involved* is the long-term goal. This means more than one event or one day. As educators and parents work together to keep an open-door policy with each other, children benefit from the strong, supportive foundation that the school and family build.

These components of parent involvement keep the process with Latino parents proceeding at a steady and active pace.

Confidence and communication are essential elements in the partnership between parents and schools. The best results happen when parents are involved in knowing what to do, and when teachers and parents respect and understand each other's roles. This is the essence of parental involvement for Latino parents.

The eight chapters in this book suggest many possible ways that educators can engage Latino parents in the education of their children.

Chapter 1: Life in Latino Families. In this chapter, I describe the heterogeneity among Latino families as well as the shared history, language, and social values, including education. According to the research, Latino families support, encourage, and assist their children through school in many ways.

Chapter 2: Latino Parent Involvement for Student Success. The parent role in the school has many faces, including those of spectators, fundraisers, and audience at meetings. But the participatory role engages parents as volunteers in the classrooms, as decision makers on curriculum matters, as personal communicators with teachers and principals, and as learners in literacy and parenting workshops that most favorably influence student academic outcomes.

Chapter 3: Sharing Information With Latino Parents. Communication is central to all parent involvement activities. Formal and informal verbal and written communication between schools and Spanish-speaking parents needs to be frequent, clear, and in the language parents best comprehend. How this is accomplished is the focus of this chapter. School conventions and procedures often require change in the school structure to facilitate systematic interchange.

Chapter 4: Parents Teaching in the Home. What parents do in the home makes a difference to students' school performance. Latino parents give their children a great deal of emotional, physical, and academic support by maintaining strong relationships with the children as well as with the school.

Chapter 5: Parents Participating in the Schools. Parent involvement programs need to be tailored to the specific community and school district. There are numerous roles parents play in the school, including that of spectators, volunteers, decision makers, and resources. Although some roles ask less of parents than decision maker, all roles are important because every one of them gets parents to the school. All contacts present opportunities for teachers to connect with Latino parents and to reach out to them and build on those interactions by inviting them to participate in particular ways.

Chapter 6: Getting Latinos to College Through Home-School Partnerships. Preparing for college begins in early elementary school by making explicit what can be a mystery and a maze for many Latino students. Latino parent involvement is immensely critical in socializing young Latino students to learn what is expected in academic achievement that leads to graduating from high school and entering college. Parent education for Latinos is an important aspect of this issue because they need to be knowledgeable about the schooling system that leads to college so that they can help students set expectations for reaching goals beyond high school.

Chapter 7: Designing Parent Involvement Programs in Schools. Whether Latino students comprise a large or small population or whether the school is largely multicultural with many different cultural groups, involving parents in the school requires a strong, well-defined program. To ensure that parent involvement is a viable part of a classroom and a school's program, educators need to construct a conscious, deliberate, and systematic process. That includes designing, implementing, and continuously assessing how Latino parents participate in their children's education and providing them with the necessary training to make them co-teachers in educating Latino students.

Chapter 8: Working With Community-Driven Organizations. Latino parents can support each other by learning from one another. Organizing themselves to support each other around educational issues has proven to be a powerful way of establishing a Latino voice in the schools. Educators can play a supportive and advocate role within the schools for community organizations that propose changes to strengthen Latino student performance.

HOW TO USE THIS BOOK

This book is organized thematically in the chapters. Within each chapter, I address the elementary and secondary needs relative to involving Latino parents in the different school levels. Much of the book is narrative, explaining the concepts in some detail under three categories: *connection, sharing information,* and *staying involved.* Throughout, I highlight *points, suggestions, personal vignettes,* and *case examples* that represent critical stop-and-reflect signposts. The boxes labeled *Point* are critical messages that are reminders to keep at a conscious level. In the boxes titled *Suggestion,* I pose ideas and activities that I have observed as successful. The suggestion boxes are labeled elementary, secondary, or both depending on where the ideas are appropriate. Some ideas apply only to elementary or to secondary schools, while other ideas apply to both school levels. These suggestions can be adapted according to the particular needs of a school or school district setting. In the *Case Example* illustrations, educators and parents reveal actual instances and practices in their parent involvement endeavors. The *Personal Vignettes* are accounts of experiences that individuals share. Whether it is a story shared by a school administrator, a parent, a teacher, community leader, or Latino student, the personal vignette is an excellent teaching tool. Personal stories have the power to convey people's emotional connection, telling how change affects their lives and how they deal with it. Where necessary, I designate the material elementary or secondary.

A special note here: The personal names that appear throughout the book are pseudonyms to protect the individuals' privacy.

ACKNOWLEDGMENTS

This book could not have been written without the generous cooperation of the many parents, children, and educators in the numerous communities where I worked. Thank you for opening up your homes and your lives and for sharing your stories with me and now with others. I am most grateful for the assistance and encouragement I received from Dr. Carmen Contreras and the San Mateo County Mother-Daughter Program. Also, special appreciation goes to Dudley Thompson for his time, support, and collaboration in the production of this book.

The contributions of the following reviewers are gratefully acknowledged:

Liliana Minaya-Rowe, Ph.D.
Professor Emeritus
Neag School of Education
University of Connecticut
Storrs, CT

Michele Dean
Principal
Montalvo Elementary
Ventura, CA

Rebecca Castro
Teacher
Montebello Unified School District
Montebello, CA

Arlene Myslinski
ESL Teacher
Buffalo Grove High School
Buffalo Grove, IL

Victoria V. Webbert
Assistant Principal for ESOL Department
Gwinnett County Public Schools
Lawrenceville, GA

Dr. Toni Griego Jones
Associate Professor
University of Arizona
Tucson, AZ

M. Elena Lopez
Senior Research Consultant
Harvard Family Research Project
Cambridge, MA

Sharon Adelman Reyes, Ph.D.
Associate Professor
Saint Xavier University
Chicago, IL

About the Author

 **Dr. Concha Delgado Gaitan** is an award-winning ethnographic researcher and scholar of oral and written traditions in immigrant communities. She relates her work with families, communities, and schools in many publications, among them her books: *The Power of Community; Literacy for Empowerment; Protean Literacy; Crossing Cultural Borders,* and *School and Society.* To her scholarly work, Dr. Delgado Gaitan brings a broad experience as an elementary school teacher, elementary school principal, ethnographic researcher, and professor of sociocultural studies at the University of California. She is currently a writer in the San Francisco Bay Area.

The genesis of this book begins with her experience as an elementary school teacher and principal. Involving the parents in every way possible prevented many problems in the classroom during the year and enhanced the classroom curriculum to more meaningfully engage the students in their learning.

As an ethnographer/researcher and professor, Dr. Delgado Gaitan once again worked in Latino communities to study family and community literacy. During these years of observing and interviewing parents, educators, and community leaders, she collaborated with them to facilitate family-school partnerships. One of the most successful efforts continues to thrive in Carpinteria, California. It has been the focus of countless articles, many national and international presentations, and a professional video, *Parents and Schools United for a Better Education,* on bridging the gap between Latino parents and the schools, which she produced. With this first-hand experience on the topic, this book offers a composite of insights, instructions, and possibilities toward sustainable partnerships between schools and Latino communities to advance Latino students' academic performance.

1

Life in Latino Families

As is true in all cultures, there is no single Latino family type. Latinos are as varied as any other ethnic group. Mexican immigrant, Mexican American, Chicano, Central American, Latin American, Puerto Rican, and Cuban: All these are identities within the Latino population in the United States. Like the cultural heterogeneity of Latino groups, the social class and socioeconomic standing also vary (Delgado-Gaitan, 1994a, 1994b). Some Latinos are U.S. born and English speaking, with heritage and history in the United States for many generations. Others are immigrants and are primarily Spanish speaking. Geographically, Latinos reside in almost every state of the union, from Florida to Alaska to Hawaii. But large concentrations of Latinos live in California, New York, Texas, Florida, Illinois, Arizona, New Jersey, New Mexico, and Colorado. About two-thirds of Latinos reside in the southwestern United States, but other states, including Wisconsin, Illinois, and Michigan, report a sizeable Latino population, while many other states have seen a growing Latino group. In some states, the Latino population is largely migratory, working in agriculture and living in temporary, substandard housing camps.

While many highly visible professionals of Latino heritage work and reside across the United States, innumerable Latinos remain relegated to working-class status as agricultural workers, factory workers, and paraprofessional service providers. Recent immigrants are most likely found in these entry-level jobs. They immigrate with high hopes of expanding educational opportunities for their children, which can lead to economic betterment. It is imperative to note that Latino workers in the United States are not just "the help" and "the leaf blowers." They are judges, architects, professors, university presidents, journalists, doctors, business owners, governors, athletes, and scientists. Latinos are Rhodes scholars and Nobel Prize winners, including Adolfo Perez, Gabriel Garcia Marquez, Octavio Paz, Rigoberta Menchu, Sergio Robles, Mario Molina, and many others. They speak not only Spanish but also English, and many speak numerous other languages as well. Officially, Latinos are the largest minority population in the United States at 37 million and 13% of the population (U.S. Bureau of the Census, 2000).

Latinos also differ with regard to the places that they call their original homeland. Although Latinos share a common heritage of language, history, and culture, differences exist within each ethnic group, ranging from the time of arrival in the United States to their socioeconomic standing. For example, both Chicanos and Mexican immigrants may be U.S. citizens, but Chicanos consider their identity a form of political consciousness and trace their ancestry to those who lived on the land that is now the Southwest, which was ceded to the United States after the Mexican-American War in 1848. The ancestors of Mexican Americans originally emigrated from Mexico during the Mexican revolution in the early 1900s. Still others with roots in Mexico are more recent immigrants.

Puerto Ricans, of course, are citizens because Puerto Rico is a U.S. territory. Three major currents of migration to the United States from Puerto Rico categorize the Puerto Rican experience. The need for workers in the United States attracted a major migration during the 1940s. An even larger migration occurred in the 1950s. Most migrated with their young families. These Puerto Ricans were skilled workers and literate in Spanish and entered the manufacturing and service industries. The third migration has been a steadier, more fluid flow of Puerto Ricans who continue to travel back and forth to Puerto Rico to work and to visit family.

Many immigrants from Central America arrived as refugees from war-torn countries including Nicaragua, El Salvador, Honduras, and Guatemala. Costa Ricans have also immigrated to the United States. Other immigrants from Latin American countries may have fled economic and social distress. Cubans arrived in two main waves from Cuba. The earlier immigrants were wealthier people fleeing the Cuban revolution, while those who came in the 1980s were people from lower socioeconomic groups in Cuba (Fuller & Olsen, 1998).

Educational attainment also differs across the Latino groups. Latino educational experience in the United States spans the continuum from low literacy to postgraduate professional education. Many complete college and graduate school; however, a large percentage of Latino students have difficulty completing high school and getting into college, especially Spanish-speaking Latinos from lower socioeconomic ranks. In some communities, Latino students drop out of school at the rate of more than 40% (National Center for Educational Statistics, 2002). Latinos have encountered prejudice and lack of access to educational resources because of their low-income status and linguistic differences.

Regardless of the Latino families' social, educational, or economic standing, they all have strengths. As in other ethnic groups, the family is the primary social unit among Latinos. Latino families also exist in many different forms, including two-parent families; extended families with grandparents, uncles, or cousins; and single-parent families. The family as a social unit holds a valued place as a resource for coping with the pressures life brings. Its preservation is critical to the continuity of social, political, religious, and cultural order. The extended family plays a very strong role. Aunts, uncles, grandparents, cousins, and family friends are frequent visitors in a Latino family household. Whether extended families live in the same home, around the corner in the same community, or in Puerto Rico, Mexico, Cuba, or Central American countries, where extended travel is required to visit, families stay close. Traditional values and practices are transmitted in families that maintain strong ties. Schools can tap these values.

Elementary and Secondary

POINT

Latino Family Values

- *Respeto.* Respect for education and educators
- *Respetar a otros.* Strong sense of mutual respect in relationships
- *Ser buen educado.* An emphasis on discipline and proper behavior
- *Compadrazgo.* The relationship between parents and godparents, translating into co-parenting

Parental authority and respect are highly valued and considered a form of love. Children are expected to take instruction from parents without questioning. Questioning parental authority is sometimes considered disrespectful, yet in some homes with high verbal deftness, it is a common practice. Latino families also expect children of all ages to learn how to maneuver successfully within the social system involving extended family members in settings where they live, study, and work.

CONNECTING

Connecting across the home-school border requires educators and Latino parents each to know the culture of the other. This happens through clear and deliberate communication. It also involves a willingness to understand and learn others' culture. The word *educación* (education) in traditional Latino families is more comprehensive than the generally accepted American usage. Although success in school becomes a valued expectation for Latino parents, the word *educación* means more than mere schooling. As used in Latino families, the term considers that the educational process is more than getting good grades in schools. It is used to describe how people comport themselves politely, how they are willing to act collectively with others, how they support and respect everyone, and how they are deferential to authority.

One Latino parent expressed it in these words: "Ignorance makes one believe that strength is in the body, not in the mind. When they think that way, they do not stop and think and negotiate with others" (translated from Spanish). In essence, the emphasis is on relationships with others in the process of achieving in school. Education is viewed as a vehicle to move children out of poverty. The desire for children to have a better life than that of the parents accounts for the sacrifices that parents make on behalf of their children.

Although their parents may be living, some Latino children have other family members as guardians, including grandparents, uncles, aunts, cousins, or older siblings, who are not the biological parents. *Educación* is part of Latino culture, and children are held to this expectation by various family members. When reaching out to Latino parents, educators need to include the students' guardian or members of the extended family who may also take charge of the children's schooling.

In Mexico and other Latin American countries, the school curriculum is very centralized. There is little choice of books, uniforms are typically required, and the school rules are firmly and uniformly set. Parents are involved in maintaining the schools and pay close attention to how well-behaved their children are. A great deal of respect is accorded to the teachers, who have a strong presence as professionals in Latino societies.

Secundaria (secondary) school is not mandatory. But for those students who can continue school after the seventh grade and don't have to drop out to work and help support their families, the first part of secondary school lasts 3 years. Following the initial *secundaria* years begins the last 3-year segment of secondary school, called *Media Superior*. It is the last 3 years of public education. Students attend for 7 hours a day and are 18 years old when they receive their diploma. Only about half of the students who complete *secundaria* continue a professional career at a university or "normal school" for teacher preparation.

Often, parents' vision of schools and education is based on their experience in their former country if they are immigrants. Part of what parents believe is necessary to support their children is to be available when the school calls.

However, for some, connecting with the schools becomes nothing less than a frustrating situation because they either do not have experience in the school system or, even if they do, they feel isolated. The school needs to hold parents in high regard. A parent, Mr. Ortiz, from a large urban school district shared this vignette with others at a parent meeting.

Elementary

POINT

Latino Parents Expect to Be Involved in Elementary Schools

- In wanting to help their children in their homework
- In staying informed about their children's academic progress
- In setting school behavior rules
- In having input in the children's discipline program
- In making decisions about their children being retained or placed in a special program

---

Secondary

PERSONAL VIGNETTE

Most of us work all day, and we're docked pay if we leave work to go to talk to the teachers. That's why we do it only in emergencies. But what happens too often is that the school calls me to tell me that my son has been in a fight or he has misbehaved and that I need to come and pick him up. I go to the school, and I'm forced to

(Continued)

(Continued)

> sit in the office and wait for longer than an hour before a secretary comes to tell me that they made a mistake. It wasn't my son after all. This has happened more than once, and I'm still trying to get to see the principal or someone to tell me why it's happening. Meanwhile, I keep losing pay when I leave my job to deal with my son's problems that aren't his.
>
> (Translated from Spanish)
>
> ---
>
> NOTE: This Personal Vignette and others in this chapter are based on interviews, observations, and case files assembled by the author over the course of a 25-year career. In some cases, names have been changed to protect privacy, but any quotations are substantially the words of the original speaker, and the incidents occurred as described.

This is one area where some Latino parents feel disconnected from the school. But nevertheless, they very much want to comply with the school's expectations and do their best to the extent of losing pay to show up at the school. The problem in this case was that the school had not made this parent's rights known to him. When parents know that they can assert their right to have the teacher, counselor, or the principal deal with them when they show up at school, their good-faith effort to work with the school is encouraged. So how can Latino parents and teachers connect?

A critical part of establishing the home-school connection is for the school to engage Latino parents in dialogue and to identify ways they can reach out to each other. Mrs. Garcia, a fourth grader's single parent, epitomizes a common sentiment on school connection. She works very late hours and sometimes cannot be at the school or talk regularly with the teacher.

Elementary

PERSONAL VIGNETTE

When I can't get to the school, I try calling the teacher from my work to check on my daughter Monica's progress in reading. But I can't always call during my break. It's important that we have personal contact with teachers because often the child is not the problem. And as long as we do not investigate the situation, our children are the ones who lose out. For me, it's important that I continue to talk to my daughter's teacher personally as often as possible about her work in the classroom, especially when I see that she's frustrated about doing homework. When I stay away, it's too easy to believe the teacher when she blames Monica for her learning problems. Then it's harder for me to help Monica at home because I don't know what's true. It would be nice for the teacher to be able to talk with me at night or even on weekends.

Like this parent, many know the value of making face-to-face contact with teachers. There is no simple formula for connecting Latino parents and teachers. Schools design their own ways of reaching out to parents, some more effective than others, but certain conditions are desirable. Latino parents already value school, and that is a critical advantage for educators to acknowledge and use as a springboard.

What educators know about Latino parents does not always include the family life: how children learn the language and culture that they bring to school. This gap in information is the source of misperceptions and generalizations about Latino families being illiterate. If students are not performing well in school, educators fault the families because they have low socioeconomic standing. Assumptions are made about the low literacy levels in the family or the low parental involvement in children's schoolwork at home. Learning how literacy exists in households is important for

Elementary and Secondary

POINT

Conditions Conducive to Latino Parents and Educators Connecting

- Latino parents value education
- Latino parents hold high expectations for their children's academic success
- Parents respect teachers' authority
- Connecting with the school is a two-way street—both parents and educators need to reach out
- Educators need to communicate parental rights in the schools to parents

educators, particularly teachers. With knowledge of the children's home life, teachers can incorporate the children's culture in the curriculum and build a stronger foundation for their academic success.

SHARING INFORMATION

Whether reading a child a bedtime story, holding family conversations in the living room, or reading correspondence from an insurance company, Latinos use language in complex ways. The heterogeneity within Latinos is reflected in the language used at home. The parents may speak Spanish while the children speak English. The matter becomes compounded when parents speak Spanish but are not literate in that language. In another language scenario, adults speak and are literate in both languages and strongly encourage their children to become fully bilingual.

Parents who are recent immigrants typically include their children in all family functions. Children's play is typically something that children do independent of adults. In the case of more educated parents, verbal engagement with children is more prominent (Heller, 1966). Talking with children is important for these families. Parents talk and sing to children from birth, or before in some cases. Siblings, uncles, aunts, grandparents, other extended family members, and friends constantly interact with children in Latino families. In some families, verbal interaction is not a high priority. When these parents become involved in parent education activities with others, they learn the importance of communicating verbally with their children. Learning to ask appropriate questions in the home is clearly a critical component of realizing parental academic expectations for their children (Heller, 1966).

Regardless of whether Spanish, English, or both languages are spoken in the home, language is a fundamental strength of Latino families. Home interactions and communication within the family are rich and full. Some families have two parents who set consistent rules for disciplining children, with strict schedules for completing their schoolwork under the careful watch of the parents or older sibling. Parents take classes in local colleges to improve their English skills and their employment opportunities. Oral and written literacy has a strong cultural and historic tradition, even in Latino families where the parents have little formal schooling. Reading materials of interest to the parents, whether these are *fotonovelas* (mininovels done with many pictures) or writing on politics and current events, are readily found around the house.

Besides their daily correspondence, families read the Bible, popular magazines, history books, poetry, personal development books, and *fotonovelas* (Laosa, 1983). Parents' workplaces influence their involvement with written literacy. Jobs require varying amounts of reading and writing. Although some jobs may not require much written literacy, they actually provide families with literacy opportunities. Some Latino immigrant women take jobs in housekeeping. They work for employers who give them not only books but mentorship about dealing with schools. In families where parents may have less written literacy skills, children still receive encouragement to do their schoolwork and to achieve. In these homes, parents rely on oral tradition to teach their children values and ways to think and perceive the world. This is a form of support for children and young adults that schools can tap and build on when engaging parents in the school's culture.

The home language and culture open children's eyes to the world, transmitting a worldview. Language and culture help define the children's identity and shape their ability to make life choices. They bring to life a family's history and world beyond the mainstream society in which they live. Language also conveys ethnic identity and pride as well as understanding of the family's position in the community.

Storytelling is still considered a popular oral tradition in Latino families. Where extended family members, including grandparents and other elders, reside with a younger family, the use of story connects the generations. Adults tell their children stories. In turn, children learn the stories and share them with peers under the carport of their apartment building or on the playground during recess. An 8-year-old boy tells the following story. It is his favorite because he learned it from his grandfather. He entitled it "Looking for a New Home."

Elementary

PERSONAL VIGNETTE

Once there was a little kitten whose name was Cloud. His owner, whose name was Anita, got sick and died. Cloud was left alone and wanted to find someone to take care of him, to feed him, bathe, and comb him. One day, Cloud left the house and got lost. Then, he was found by an older man who told him that he wanted to help him cross the street. Then they became friends and the kitten, Cloud, was happy.

(Translated from Spanish)

Not all stories are original. Parents may be more familiar with popular stories. Some parents tell their children adaptations of classics such as the "Three Little Pigs" and "Little Red Riding Hood," weaving contemporary plots into the traditional story line. Without question, this language-learning activity teaches storytelling techniques while providing an opportunity to listen and pose questions. Regardless of the story, children and parents revel in their time together. When reaching out to Latino parents, it is critical for educators to recognize the parents' willingness to know about their children's academic progress. What deters their active participation can be addressed structurally through well-designed programs.

What Latino children bring to school is who they are, what they believe, how they feel, and how they behave in a culture that is rich in history, language, values, customs, and practices. Of importance is the information that educators and parents share about the less visible cultural practices that underlie interactions in the family and in the school. Family unity is a strong value in the way that families serve as resource for each other. Sometimes, Latino families are thought to be overly dependent on each other. In Latino families, the practice of interdependence is highly valued. As Latino families remain in the United States for longer periods of time and as they advance into higher education, gain facility in English, and move into the professions, students lose their primary language. However, this fact does not necessarily distance them from their culture. They remain close to other aspects of their culture through networks established with other members of the cultural group. Family networks reveal the value of interdependence across the multiple generations of Latinos in the United States.

The word *cooperative* is often used to describe Latino conduct, especially for children in the schools. Sometimes, their behavior is misinterpreted, and children are stereotyped as passive. But the word *collective* is more appropriate when addressing preferred behavior of Latino children because it describes their ability to join with others in a group activity.

There is also a collective character to the concept of interdependence that allows individuals to give and receive support. Interdependence as a practice and value in Latino families has much to do with the person's role as an active, sharing family member. It does not necessarily mean that people are dependent on others in a way that renders them irresponsible. In fact, interdependence in older children and adults is characterized by an expectation of performing household duties and supporting others.

ACROSS GENERATIONS OF LATINOS

The issue of parent involvement of Latino families in the schools is not limited to recent immigrants or to parents who have limited English and whose children are at risk academically. The majority of Latinos are U.S. citizens who have resided in this country for generations and whose primary language is English. In fact, some no longer speak Spanish, yet their experience with the schooling system has been one of estrangement and conflict. Although some have traversed the home-school divide and have gone on to succeed academically through public elementary and secondary schools and colleges, all too many have a schooling experience characterized by prejudice and inequity. The important point here is that Latino participation in the schools cannot be won by simply translating everything from English to Spanish. The issue is more than what language is spoken. It has to do with attitude on the part of the school toward the underrepresented Latino community. Schools must be willing to reach out in culturally appropriate ways, to make an effort to include Latino students in special academic enhancement programs supporting their achievement, and to integrate Latino cultural contributions in the school curriculum.

Generations of historical, social, and cultural distance between the schools and the Latino community must be bridged. This is possible only through systematic outreach to Latino community leaders, to Latino religious and social organizations, and to every Latino family to make them an integral part of the decision-making voice

---

Elementary and Secondary

POINT

The School Culture That Latino Parents Need to Know

- *Individualism.* Students are expected to think for themselves
- *Independence.* Students are expected to work on their own
- *Promptness.* Students are expected to arrive at class or meetings on time

---

of the school on a regular basis. This must extend beyond a one-time token invitation to attend a music assembly on Cinco de Mayo. The effort must be a part of the school's daily activity plan. The activities in this book are not limited to engaging Spanish-speaking Latino parents. The points made, the case examples illustrated, and the suggestions offered include but extend beyond the type of English/Spanish language differences between the home and the school.

School Culture

Schools, like families, have a way of conducting business day in and day out. There's a language that organizes the classroom, and it is something that parents need to learn.

The school culture is reflected in the classroom. Working independently is highly valued by most teachers, as is the focus on the individual. Promptness and efficiency are also expected in all activities.

The school culture can create and communicate an open, positive, and welcoming environment, or it can convey a closed, defensive, and unwelcoming place for parents to contact and visit. What parents and teachers know about the culture of the home and the culture of the school, respectively, is the foundation on which to build a continuing relationship for the benefit of the children's academic achievement.

Elementary and Secondary

POINT

Family Values That Latino Parents Bring to School

- *Language.* Spanish and English
- *Collectivity.* Strength in joining with others
- *Interdependence.* Strongly support others

STAYING INVOLVED

Adversity

At some time or another, all families face turmoil and difficulty, and certainly Latino families are no exception. They experience travail with greater frequency because of the conditions in which they live. The pain of unemployment, underemployment, health crisis, divorce, substance abuse, and teenage school dropouts can overwhelm families. Maintaining a healthy family becomes increasingly difficult. In crowded apartments with large families, households fill with despair, especially if alcoholism overloads the situation. Members of these families often live with a gag over their mouths because of the shame and isolation they feel. For many Latino children who live in these families, going to school is their only release from a fear-filled environment. Many children who come from homes lacking money, security, and encouragement fail to adjust to a new culture in the school. Concentration and energy to learn are almost impossible for these children.

Unresponsive schools may compound the situation of poverty until they work with parents to interrupt the cycle (Fuller & Olsen, 1998). Parents find support for dealing with their social problems through community agencies. Where social isolation pertaining to their children's schooling is concerned, it becomes even more critical for educators to provide avenues for parents to share their frustrations and strengths while getting involved in the schools (Lareau, 2000). Taking advantage of access to resources often means having community support groups that assist others to make necessary social changes. For children coming from stress-filled homes, positive school experiences play an even stronger role in their lives. Educators need to design programs that will systematically advocate for children as they attempt to learn under the pressures of their daily lives.

Typically, parents of higher socioeconomic background participate more regularly in the schools even if the schools do not encourage parent involvement (Epstein, 1994). Their familiarity with the school system makes it easier for them to know how to involve themselves. However, some educational institutions believe that parents who have not been educated in the United States, or who speak only Spanish, are deficient in their ability to support their children in education. Schools need to acknowledge the families' cultural strengths. Educators do this by incorporating family strengths into the school curriculum. By recognizing and developing pride in their identity, schools let parents know they can provide valuable contributions. When schools recognize that families bring the strength of resilience, students are advantaged as their parents' resourcefulness is taken into account.

As is the case with living in a culturally different home, speaking Spanish need not be a disability to parent participation. Latino families may draw a boundary between the school and the home because they respect the teachers' authority and hand over full authority for their children's education to the school. Trusting the teacher to know what is best for their children is important, but it sometimes interferes with parents becoming advocates for their children on a regular basis. Within the home, parents provide for physical and emotional needs.

SUMMARY

- There is no single prototype of a Latino family. Latino families are as varied as families in every other cultural group.
- In spite of different neighborhoods where they reside, their varying educational attainment, and the amount of Spanish and English spoken at home, the level of literacy used in the home, and the way that they involve themselves in their children's schooling, all families have strengths.
- The linguistic and cultural differences of Latinos are not deficits; rather, they are valuable strengths and knowledge that benefit the students' academic performance.
- Latino families' strengths manifest in the history, language, cultural values, and expectations for their children's success.
- Their day-to-day interactions in the family make it possible for Latino families to continuously grow, adjust, and change.

2

Connecting Latino Parents to the Classroom

That parent involvement benefits Latino students' educational success goes without saying. Educators that work collaboratively with Latino parents find students perform better academically. More than parental level of education, family size, or family's socioeconomic level, the extent to which schools reach out to establish parent involvement in ethnically diverse schools is the strongest determinant of Latinos getting involved in their children's education. In both elementary and secondary education, a major tenet in the parent participation issue is that parent involvement is not a problem. It is a rich resource, a tool, much like a book that informs us and moves us toward our destination.

Too often, educators in schools with large ethnic and culturally different groups perceive the situation as a problem because they believe the stereotype—that language or cultural differences interfere with learning. This occurs when we see differences in culture, ethnicity, or social class as a deficit. Labeling parents "problematic" or "hard to reach" makes relating to Latino communities even more difficult by placing the burden of communicating and getting involved on the parents rather than examining the educational system to evaluate its weakness relative to parent involvement.

In schools where parent involvement has been systematic, persistent, and well organized, student achievement improves. A great deal of research in recent decades confidently claims the importance of parent involvement relative to student academic achievement. Even in diverse communities that are typically underrepresented in the schools, there is evidence that parent involvement impacts student achievement (Aspiazu, Bauer, & Spillett 1998; Decker & Decker, 2003; Delgado-Gaitan, 2001).

Reaching out to the Latino community is a matter of building trust as a platform for creating sustained collaborations with parents. Latino families need to know that educators are interested in meeting their needs and are respectful of their language and cultural differences (Henderson & Mapp, 2002). When educators reach out to Latino communities, each group's perceptions of the other shape and influence how they relate to each other. It is important to remember this when trying to involve Latino parents in the school. Latino parents who have little contact with professionals such as educators may feel self-conscious and limited in their ability to discuss schooling in terms unfamiliar to them. Therefore, whether the contact is personal in the home, at school, or by phone, educators need to be conscious of the fact that all parents know something about the most important topic at hand: their child. Thus, educators need to make the parents feel at ease and win their trust in order to engage them in an ongoing conversation.

Both elementary and secondary educators need to remember that regardless of culture, educational attainment, and socioeconomic standing, all families have strengths, and educators can tap that potential to maximize student achievement. When they drop their barriers and fears, educators who once believed that the Spanish-speaking community presented a problem because its members spoke different languages can become convinced that working with the Latino community is possible.

Principal Kim Lambert speaks of her experience as an elementary school principal in a small city school district. She had been a principal in the school district for a few years and went about her business quite effortlessly until she realized that the student population in her school was changing. Within a year, the Spanish-speaking Latino students gradually became the majority in her school. Ms. Lambert describes the change in her school that transformed her way of thinking, from fearing the Latino families to becoming a strong advocate for them.

Elementary

PERSONAL VIGNETTE

It's like I was working hard with my head down on the page and when I looked up, the entire complexion of the school had changed. When I first realized that I had such a large Latino population in the school and that I couldn't speak their language, I felt shut out. I was sad and scared. It seemed as though I was isolated from them. Most of the time that I had to speak with a parent, we met with one of the bilingual teacher assistants that translated. And then I realized that it must be the way that they feel about having to relate to a school where most of the teachers and the administrators don't speak Spanish.

Then I learned that the Latino parents had been holding meetings with every principal in the district. I didn't know what I would say to them or how we would communicate. Fortunately, one of the directors from the central office attended the meeting with the Latino parents, and he translated. Except for the fact that I felt so limited in my ability to talk spontaneously and explain everything I had to say, I felt so privileged to know these people. They were decent, caring, and intelligent people who wanted more than anything in the world to have the best for their children.

At the end of the meeting they made a couple of requests that hadn't occurred to me as something that they would need. At the top of the list was to have all communication sent to them bilingually. Somehow I just figured that they could get someone to read the English to them if they couldn't read it. What a ludicrous thing to believe. But thank goodness that the parents just made everything so clear to me. It all made sense how I needed to do my part as a principal to communicate with them so that neither they nor I felt isolated from each other. We're in this together and need to communicate as fully as possible because we have the children's academic future in our hands.

NOTE: This Personal Vignette and others in this chapter are based on interviews, observations, and case files assembled by the author over the course of a 25-year career. In some cases, names have been changed to protect privacy, but any quotations are substantially the words of the original speaker, and the incidents occurred as described.

Just as Principal Lambert found it imperative to learn about her school community even after she had been there for several years, so do new elementary and secondary teachers need to become acquainted with the community in which they teach. Learning about the language, beliefs, and cultural practices of Latino students enhances communication and prevents potential misunderstanding. If teachers do not delay contact until they have to make a negative report to the parents about the student's academic standing, they have a better chance to resolve a problem to the student's advantage.

At the high school level, fear of involving Latino parents in the school is manifested similarly, but some things differ. As is the case in the personal vignette below with a high school teacher who teaches in an inner-city high school, relating to Latino parents needs to be systematized. Mr. Brink is a teacher of English in a class designed to teach English-Language Learners (ELL).

Secondary

PERSONAL VIGNETTE

What I find problematic is that whenever the school needs to communicate with Latino parents, they always call on me or the other English teacher who teaches classes for English–Language Learners. No one else seems to feel that it's their responsibility to deal with Spanish-speaking Latino parents. Yes, there are Latino parents who speak English quite well and don't require translators, but the problem is beyond the language, it seems to me. Because other personnel don't spend as much time with Latino students as I do in my classes, they just push off any difficulty that Latino parents have in the schools to me. There's a need for the entire school to assume responsibility for educating and learning about the Latino students' culture as well as their parents. If it's just us who teach ELL students that take any interest in their families, the students will never have all the support they need from the school. And most of these students have many issues that require us to have close contact with parents. And it needs to be the responsibility of the entire school to deal with Latino parents in a way that they can support us to help the students' academic progress. The entire school needs to be involved in embracing the Latino culture and communicating as much as possible with students as well as the parents.

The limited outreach to Latino parents that Mr. Brink describes at this high school is frustrating at best. Fear and indifference on the part of schools in working with Latino parents create large gaps in communication and loss of opportunities for Latino students to advance in their academic program. In the absence of a systematic parent-involvement program, parents fail to receive the information they need, and some teachers, like Mr. Brink, are burdened by having to be the only ones to do the work necessary. However, in some cases, a situation like this one can be reversed. The teachers who know the community best can enlist the assistance of some Latino parents and then have them communicate with other parents. United, the parents can proceed as other community-driven groups have done to get the cooperation of the school and have their needs met. There is more discussion on community-driven efforts in subsequent chapters.

UNDERSTANDING PARENT INVOLVEMENT

How parent involvement is organized and practiced varies from area to area across this country, depending on the school personnel who create educational policy as well as the interpretation by the community that the schools serve. Regardless of how each school and community defines parent involvement, one consistent purpose stands out.

Defining parent involvement with a broad stroke, we can include the family's role in the home in this process, as well as participation in school activities. This broad framework is sufficiently ample to incorporate traditional and nontraditional activities. In more traditional forms of parent involvement, the schools organize and orchestrate the activities, rendering parents passive. Conventional parent-involvement activities in the schools engage parents in raising funds, attending teacher-parent conferences, and supplying input on selective decisions when requested by the principals.

Nontraditional activities are more apt to be co-designed by parents and teachers and involve parents as active participants. These include the parental role and school-related activities in the home.

Nonconventional parent-involvement activities occupy parents in stronger roles and as a more consistent presence in the schools. Parents attend and lead bilingual workshops on strengthening the parental role in children's education. Schools take proactive measures to prevent academic and social crises. Parents are continuously informed in Spanish about their children's classroom academic progress. Parents and teachers make decisions on the schools' curriculum. Child care is offered to parents attending meetings and workshops.

Traditional activities have been easier for the schools to implement because the schools take charge, and these activities have been institutionalized for so many years that they become automatic and routine for schools to organize. In traditional activities, schools do not feel that it is necessary to accommodate parents. Nontraditional activities are often more effective in helping parents, through training and participation, to grow and gain valuable knowledge about the school and their children.

For schools to design effective parent-involvement activities and programs, they have to provide various levels of involvement, which operate continuously. Three basic levels of influence in students' academic lives include the family, the school, and the community. Fundamentally, what happens in the family is crucial to students' learning from the time children are born through their school career. Not only are basic cultural values and beliefs learned in the family, but also daily practices often speak louder than words. In the Latino family, if parents are not directly active in their child's schooling, educators could perceive this to be a case of indifference toward the school. But what may be driving their behavior is fear or lack of understanding of their role in the school system. They may feel that they are doing the best they can already by caring for their children's basic needs in the home. So they need to be taught how to make the fourth point of this graphic a reality.

Elementary and Secondary

POINT

Family Responsibility
Toward Education

- Provide physical needs
- Provide emotional and psychological support
- Provide instruction in values
- Provide advocacy in schools

In addition to the psycho-emotional familial support, the family is also responsible for assisting the student with schoolwork. The school has its own set of obligations toward encouraging parent involvement, including educating parents about school programs and facilitating English literacy so that parents can better assist their children.

Latino parents from poor communities are often criticized for not participating in schools. Limited ability to speak English, lack of familiarity with the mainstream culture, and social class standing are often blamed for their children's underachievement. Ultimately, this is translated as the parents not valuing education and not caring about their children's schooling. Parents, in turn, claim that they don't have enough time, they don't feel welcome in school, they don't speak English, they don't understand the school system, they don't have child care, and they don't have transportation. While all of these may actually prevent some Latino parents from being active in the school, in reality, many of these issues are not culturally related. The reasons that keep Latino parents out of the schools are primarily structural. How the schools and parent involvement programs are organized determines whether Latino parents are included and are able to participate or not.

There are as many goals for parent involvement as there are parents and teachers working toward those ends. But two salient goals merit mentioning here because they are critical to the importance of having Latino families involved in the schools. First, achieving parent involvement is an ongoing process with the goal of including parents in the decision making about their children's education. Parents' strengths are

---

Elementary and Secondary

POINT

Parent Involvement Is . . .

. . . a process, a context, and set of activities to support and socialize students with school through systematic connection between the home and the school. Engaging Latino parents in the schools means establishing three principles for interacting:

- Authentic interest
- Trust
- Respect

Elementary and Secondary

POINT

The Mission of Latino Parent Involvement Is . . .

- To maximize and promote opportunities for Latino students from preschool level through high school to achieve to their potential, graduate, and enter college
- To create parent involvement programs that have this objective as the leading motivation and end

recognized through continuous dialogue between them and educators. Parents and school personnel together can transform practices and policies related to Spanish-speaking Latino children. Inherent in this process is the conviction that all individuals have strengths and that learning new roles occurs through negotiation and participation in new social arrangements.

The reason for the first goal is to reach the second goal, which is to improve the students' academic achievement. Although there is evidence that test scores do not increase as a result of parent involvement, we need to think in much broader terms about achievement. Day-to-day academic performance is much more complex than test scores. It is in this non-test arena that the personal fruits of parent involvement are most apparent. That is where we begin to perceive positive student attitudes toward school, disciplined behaviors in completing schoolwork and out of school, ability to persist against adversity, and social intelligence to rally support in school from friends and adults.

3

Sharing Information With Latino Parents

Communication between educators and parents consists of more than merely translating into Spanish the information that the school wants Latino parents to know. True communication occurs when parents and teachers strive for a meaningful exchange around topics that affect children's learning. The crux of communication rests on the willingness of both sides to listen to the other's position and negotiate a win-win solution.

To fully support Latino student learning, parents and teachers need to communicate frequently. Different types of communication, depending on the need, can be short-term or long-term, a one-time issue or an extended situation. Whatever the need, communication between educators and Latino parents must be ongoing and remain consistent to the mission of ensuring academic success of Latino students. Although parents are much more involved on a continuous basis in the elementary grades, parents of secondary Latino students also need to communicate frequently with the schools; the needs change across the grades, but the purpose and outcomes remain the same: to support children's and youth's schooling experience. Through continuous communication between parents and teachers, educational issues can be discussed and resolved before they escalate and create learning problems for the student.

How the school setting and culture is organized makes a great deal of difference in the way that Latino parents participate in the schools. In elementary as well as secondary schools, Latino parents tell of feeling unwelcome. Barriers to communication can be eliminated in three major ways. First, the school needs to provide inservice training for teachers and other educators who deal with Latino families on how to communicate with parents. Second, teachers can give parents a resource handbook with names of bilingual staff in the school district whom they can contact to deal with various educational concerns. Third, making the school a warm and welcoming place makes it easier for parents to drop in as needed.

What the school says to Latino parents when they enter the grounds makes a great deal of difference as to whether they feel welcome or not. If schools fail to hire a bilingual person for the front office, or if schools do not translate written correspondence into Spanish, the message sent to parents is one of indifference toward the community. When this occurs, Latino parents are inclined to stay away from the school. Therefore, the first step in involving Latino parents is to value Latino parents' language by employing office personnel who can communicate with them by phone and who can translate correspondence that goes to the families.

CONNECTING

Teacher-parent exchange affirms parents' interest in working with teachers and their need to meet and talk about ways to support their children. One parent, Mrs. Sosa, describes how, by communicating with her third-grade son's teacher and other parents, she learned to communicate better with her son. Her story was originally told in Spanish and translated to English.

Elementary

CASE EXAMPLE

As parents we get together weekly or bimonthly at the community center and discuss our children's education. It was in meetings with this group of parents that I learned how important it was for me to communicate with my son's teacher the entire time even when he was doing well. For it was important to talk almost daily with my son Mario's teacher, Ms. Mora. In my conversation with the teacher, I feel supported and can express my ideas any time. At first, I didn't think that his teacher paid attention to Mario, and she didn't think I cared either. But we were willing to talk and find out where we differed and where we agreed. What has helped me most is that the teacher has taken the time to help me learn how to help Mario. It has made me more confident about what teachers teach our children. Now, I feel better about trusting that the teachers are disciplining our children in the way that we as Latino parents expect. I would say that when we work together, the children have more support. Mario has shown some real progress since his teacher and I have been communicating more often. By talking with Ms. Mora, I've learned how to love and discipline him at home so that he understands that his schooling interests me and [that] how he progresses does matter to me, that [I want him to] feel comfortable and confident about his own academic studies. Now he stays occupied with his schoolwork and he actually finishes it because I think he knows that his teacher and I agree on what's good for him.

NOTE: This Case Example and others in this chapter are based on interviews, observations, and case files assembled by the author over the course of a 25-year career. In some cases, names have been changed to protect privacy, but any quotations are substantially the words of the original speaker, and the incidents occurred as described.

Mrs. Sosa clearly highlights the significance of continuous connection with her son's teacher as well as with other parents. For Latino parents who are unaccustomed to working with schools, uniting informally with other Latino parents informs them and helps to break misconceptions about schools. Culturally instilled notions of education are easier to change when members of the same cultural group supply information.

Elementary

SUGGESTION

Making Parents Welcome in Elementary Schools Begins By . . .

- Being willing to reach out to Latino parents through their language and culture
- Employing bilingual office personnel where needed in the school
- Listening to parents' concerns
- Negotiating a win-win solution

In communication with Latino parents, secondary schools face a problem similar to the one that elementary schools confront. That is, educators often communicate with parents only to relay a negative message. Secondary schools, like elementary schools, must make communicating with Latino parents a priority. The following vignette illustrates Mr. Ramirez's frustration in dealing with a high school in a small school district that did not have a plan to communicate with Spanish-speaking Latino parents. He shared this with other Latino parents at a Migrant Education Program meeting.

Parental isolation and frustration as a result of noncommunication between schools and Latino parents adversely affects the students.

Secondary

PERSONAL VIGNETTE

Sometimes that high school makes me so frustrated. I don't understand how they expect me to work with my son, Alfredo, when they don't tell me what the problem is. My son is now in the 10th grade, but the problems have been going on since last year. He's gotten into fights a couple of times, and the school calls me to come and pick him up. So I leave my work and go get him. But I can never talk with the principal, who is never there. I don't know why the school can't discipline him when they have him. I only went to school in the first grade in Mexico, and I don't read or write, so all of this stuff having to do with the school makes me very nervous. The worst case happened last Friday when the school called me at work to come and pick up Alfredo. I came to the school and waited in the office, and they couldn't find where my son was. Neither was the principal there. The secretary didn't know what the problem was, and she couldn't help me. So I waited for over an hour-and-a-half until the principal arrived. It turned out that they had the wrong Latino boy's name and it wasn't my son after all. It was someone else. There's got to be some way to stop this, but I don't know how to do it alone. I need other parents who are more experienced to help me deal with the schools.

NOTE: This Personal Vignette and others in this chapter are based on interviews, observations, and case files assembled by the author over the course of a 25-year career. In some cases, names have been changed to protect privacy, but any quotations are substantially the words of the original speaker, and the incidents occurred as described.

Certainly, communicating with Latino parents of high school students is a challenge. But it is imperative for educators and parents to work together and ensure that Latino high school students excel in their academics, graduate, and get into college. Two issues compound Mr. Ramirez's interactions with the school. He speaks limited English, and he does not know the language of the school. Like many Latino parents, he does not know how to navigate through the school when problems arise, much less how to prevent them.

Secondary

SUGGESTION

Making Parents Welcome in Secondary Schools Begins by...

- Assigning bilingual educators to communicate with parents on a regular basis
- Calling and writing to parents to report on students' strengths and progress as needed

Whether the school is small or large, in an urban setting or not, secondary schools need to recognize the urgency of communicating systematically with Latino parents in a way that ensures that parents comprehend and exercise their rights and responsibilities. Schools need to identify a bilingual teacher, counselor, or administrator in the school who can contact and communicate with Latino parents at all times. If a bilingual educator is unavailable, the school needs to hire a person to translate conferences, meetings, and other communications with parents.

INFORMAL VERBAL CONTACTS WITH PARENTS

A wise person once said, "I never learned anything important when I was talking." What this means is that listening opens doors to important knowledge. Knowing how, what, and where to communicate and recognizing some of the pitfalls inherent in forging such communication are important considerations for teachers working with Latino parents. The primary focus of all communication is listening. Effective listening is the starting point of all interpersonal communication with Latino parents. Listen for the intent of the message. After the person has spoken, paraphrase what is said without changing the meaning. Accept the person's comment without judgment. Then, without evaluating the person's communication, begin a response about the message. To listen with understanding, teachers and any other personnel in contact with Latino parents need to be bilingual. Like all other parents, Latino parents want to feel heard. Usually, when we stop listening, when we want things only our way, when we think we're right, we can't make inclusive decisions that lead to empowerment in the community. Teachers and other educators making contact with Latino parents can establish a strong basis for communicating through active listening.

The question becomes, What is it that educators and parents are listening for to learn from each other? Fundamentally, ways to best assist children in their learning is the key body of knowledge that educators and parents need to share. Essentially, Latino children's behavior, skills, and attitudes interrelate. Latino children's intelligence and achievement rest on numerous factors. Their motivation, collectivity, and confidence influence their effort and initiative. Focusing on and completing their schoolwork takes responsibility, perseverance, and caring (Ames, DeStefano, Watkins, & Sheldon, 1995b). Addressing how Latino children perform in all these achievement indicators in the classroom and at home maximizes their opportunity to succeed in school.

In communities where children walk to school, many Latino parents make it a point to walk with them. They take that opportunity to talk with the teacher and check in about their child's progress. These small interactions may seem unimportant, but to many parents, they are extremely meaningful exchanges. They are occasions that both parents and teachers appreciate because they can clarify homework questions, classroom behavior reports, and ways to support their children at home. However, these quick exchanges are only possible when there is an educator in the classroom who can talk with parents in Spanish. If a Spanish-speaking teacher is not available to teach their child and to speak to them in a language they understand, the parents tend to withdraw from the school. They take the lack of a Spanish-speaking teacher to mean that the school is not only unwelcoming but also uncaring. The school, in turn, interprets the parents' absence as apathy. What educators need to do to encourage parents to drop in and to pay attention to phone calls and written correspondence is to address them in Spanish and in comprehensible language, not educational jargon. Explaining a school-related problem, concern, or situation to Latino parents who are unfamiliar with school language requires that educators use language that conveys the message clearly, but not condescendingly.

SHARING INFORMATION

Home Talk in the School

Talk in the home has important implications for educators, especially teachers. Families share many activities in the home that contribute to the children's orientation to the world and their place in it. Parents use day-to-day events to socialize their children and teach them values, such as the importance of education, to communicate with other members of the family, to support and shape their children's understanding, and to demonstrate family cohesion.

The way parents share time with their children in a Latino home sheds light on ways for educators to communicate with parents. In this personal vignette, family photos bring together the parents and children to consider their family history.

Elementary

PERSONAL VIGNETTE

In this scene, the mother showed family pictures to three of her children, Juan, Elena, and Bobby, ages 12, 10, and 7, respectively.

Mother: Look at these pictures. Do you remember who these kids are?

Elena: My cousins.

Mother: In Michoacan. Do you know where that is?

All: In Mexico.

Elena: Why do they live there?

Mother: Because their parents have a ranch over there. Do you remember when we visited there 2 years ago?

Bobby: No, I don't.

Mother: That's because you were very small. You were just a baby.

All: [looking at another picture] Grandma.

Mother: Would you like to visit her at her ranch again?

Elena: I would. I like the animals.

(Continued)

(Continued)

Mother:	What else do you remember about the ranch?
All:	Horses and chickens and lots of things.
Mother:	Would you like to live there?
Juan:	No, it's really boring because they don't have TV or movie theaters.
Mother:	That's true, but it's because you've become accustomed to living here in the United States.

What is communicated in this seemingly small interaction is the children's interest in remaining in the United States. This was probably something that the mother had already surmised. After all, the children had become accustomed to the conveniences in this country. The daughter, however, expressed interest in visiting her cousins and the ranch in Mexico.

Not only is knowledge of communication in the home valuable in the classroom, but it can also inform the way that teachers communicate with parents. For example, teachers can inquire about how parents interact with children during conversations other than talk about schoolwork. Knowing about communication in the home can assist teachers in planning the language and literacy curriculum. It is equally necessary for parents to know the ways that communication occurs in the classroom.

Parent-child interaction develops listening and conversation skills. If children are not heard, they will find some way to get attention at home and in school, often through negative behavior. They want to be heard. Teachers can gain insights about the children's home learning environment in conversations with parents.

Elementary

SUGGESTION

Building on Home Communication—Some Questions to Ask Parents

- What recent conversations have you had with your child that were not necessarily about homework?
- What kinds of questions does your child ask you?

How the child expresses feelings at home can tell the teacher if the home is a place for loving relationships. How parents communicate with children impacts discipline at school. How parents and children talk with each other at home, whether the parents use only directives to talk to the children, or whether children are invited to ask questions can inform classroom curriculum decisions.

VISITING FAMILIES

The home visit provides an opportunity for educators and parents to get to know each other and talk informally about the student's interests and needs. However, in recent years, making home visits as a means of face-to-face, teacher-parent communication has decreased. Concerns about invading family privacy, finding parents unavailable at home due to work schedules, and creating overworked teachers all interfere with home visits as a means of engaging Latino parents in their children's schooling. Nevertheless, the value of face-to-face interaction cannot be underestimated.

When making home visits, school personnel, whether teacher, teacher assistant, or community liaison, need to use the preferred home language and respect the family's time constraints and their choice of location, whether their home, the community center, or a church hall. With these things in mind, school personnel can hold productive and informative meetings.

Home visits serve children's learning and the teacher's educational plan in two significant ways. First, they anticipate problems before they flare up in the classroom because parents and teachers agree on their respective expectations in advance. Second, when problems do flare up and teachers meet parents on their home front and in person, they can resolve issues that are difficult to handle through phone or written communications.

Those parents who cannot make it to school or who may feel intimidated by the school setting can be reached through the home visit. For some teachers, visiting each child's home is just part of their routine. They set aside part of a Saturday to do it instead of making visits in the evenings. Other teachers visit the students before school begins in the fall to solicit parental support and express the need for parents to work along with the school during the year. Teachers learn about the children's strengths, as well as those of their families, and they find ways to incorporate the home culture in the day-to-day curriculum.

FOCUS GROUPS

In small focus groups, educators can meet personally with Latino parents to discuss topics of concern to everyone. Raising critical questions with parents in a small group is an effective way of getting parents to have discussions with others. They learn how other parents are thinking and feeling concerning children, school, homework, peer pressure, discipline, careers, college plans, or any other topic (Jayanthi & Nelson, 2002).

> *Elementary*
>
> ## SUGGESTION
>
> ## Informal Forms of Communication
>
> - Phone calls
> - Notes sent home
> - Chats with parents at classroom door
> - Home visits
> - Informal focus groups on selected topics

How high school educators stay connected to Latino parents varies depending on the personnel in charge of communicating with parents. Some high schools link parents with family community agencies, community businesses, and colleges to keep them informed about ways to support students and to access resources to strengthen their achievement.

WRITTEN CORRESPONDENCE

After a personal meeting with a parent about a sensitive issue, some teachers find it important to write a letter or note to the parent to reinforce what was discussed and how it was resolved. Formal written contact sent home to Latino parents through report cards and newsletters needs to be bilingual. An issue that parents raise is that written communication sent to them should be translated completely, not just summarized. Yes, translation is important, but communication between parents and educators means more than merely translating English to Spanish. It means ensuring that the purpose of the communication is delivered.

LANGUAGE AT MEETINGS

Translation for parents needs to be available at school parent meetings such as back to school nights and site council meetings, as well as during meetings of PTA groups where such groups exist. For many Latino parents, back to school night is an easier event to attend than others; they can be part of an audience without being required to interact much.

Parent-teacher conferences need to be conducted bilingually. It is imperative to have an interpreter at parent-teacher conferences if the teacher does not speak Spanish. Although some teachers have the students act as translators because they are more fluent in English than their parents, it is best for a bilingual school employee to interpret if the teacher does not speak Spanish.

Speaking Spanish is not the only consideration when communicating with Latino parents. When educators use professional terminology, their language can sound unfamiliar, even to parents who are native English speakers. As a result, many Latino parents whose experi-

---

Elementary and Secondary

SUGGESTION

To Ensure Making Contact With Parents . . .

- Use Spanish when calling the home
- Translate written materials sent to the home
- Offer child care to parents for scheduled meetings, workshops, and events
- Have Spanish–speaking personnel available to speak to parents when they come to school
- Request a response from the parents to assure that they have understood, and solicit their ideas

---

Elementary and Secondary

POINT

Formal Forms of Communication

- Back to school night
- Site council meetings
- PTA meetings
- Weekly (school or classrooms) newsletters to parents
- Quarterly parent–teacher conference
- Quarterly grade report cards

---

rience with the schools has been minimal or negative feel intimidated when meeting with educators. Whether the communication is spoken or written, whether the language is English or Spanish, it is important for educators to use a common language that parents can understand. This seventh-grade math teacher, Mr. Simons, demonstrates how educational jargon can interfere with comprehension of classroom business even when teachers are talking with English-speaking Latino parents.

Secondary

CASE EXAMPLE

Be sure one is communicating information and not fear. In open-house meetings, teachers should talk to parents about the classroom and school curriculum in terms they understand. An example:

This is a state adoption year in our math program. Our school has decided to adopt the Houghton Mifflin books after reviewing several programs. The basic feature of this program is that it requires the students to read a great deal in performing the activities. All the high-level patterns, tables, graphs, and variables are items that standardized tests require students to know.

Seventh-grade math teacher

When Making Such a Presentation, Ask Yourself

- Do parents know what *state adoption* means?
- Are they familiar with the way schools review curricula and textbooks?
- Do they understand the relationship between curriculum and standardized tests?
- Have you asked them if they understand what the terminology means?

Although Mr. Simons wants to inform the Latino parents in his classroom, he makes the mistake of thinking that because they speak English, they're familiar with an educator's professional terminology. Sometimes, Latino parents feel embarrassed to acknowledge that they don't know what the teacher means. Therefore, it is best to take the safe road and explain everything in comprehensible terms. Lessons for dealing with such issues come from many communities where parents and teachers attempt to communicate with each other. One such case follows with Mrs. Sierra and her daughter's fifth-grade teacher.

Elementary

CASE EXAMPLE

In the case of fifth grader Paula, her mother, Mrs. Sierra, and her teacher, Mrs. Thomas, discuss how Paula's literacy skills have declined. The conversation is translated from Spanish.

Mother: I'm having a problem with Paula, who doesn't want to do her homework on reading.

Teacher: What kind of problem do you have with her?

Mother: Well, every night when she should be doing her homework, she doesn't want to do it. I get very angry, and she even trembles. I don't understand why. I know she's a very good student in math.

Teacher: Yes, Paula is a pretty good student in math, but it's possible that she has lost some confidence in reading because she is in a more advanced group.

Mother: Shouldn't she have more confidence if she's in a higher group?

Teacher: She was doing well here in the classroom until recently. Maybe what is going on when she does her homework has something to do with it?

Mother: It's possible that I'm overly strict with her because I am too anxious about reading. Math is not as difficult for me because I always liked the subject, and I could compute, but where reading was concerned, I have never excelled.

Teacher: Paula is a very good student in math, and it's possible that she's picked up your attitude about math and feels more support with that subject. That has helped her to do well in it.

Mother: You're right. Maybe I can just wait for her to ask for assistance rather than forcing her to listen to the way I want her to do her reading homework.

Elementary and Secondary

POINT

Common Language for Formal and Informal Occasions

- Practice effective listening
- Conduct meetings bilingually
- Make frequent contact
- Speak to parents in comprehensible language
- Present possibilities
- Speak to parents' strengths

Teachers and parents sometimes fear each other. They reach out to each other in the way they know best, but if their communication fails to produce a solution that they expect, they may feel that the other party is not cooperating. Therefore, when parents and teachers communicate with each other, the language that they use needs to be meaningful.

STAYING INVOLVED

Parents and teachers agree that they need to communicate with each other, and both sides claim their share of limitations when they work apart. Sharing knowledge and respect for cultural practices with each other helps parents and teachers reach an understanding.

Latino parents, however, need to be drawn into a sustained connection with the school. The reverse is also true; Latino parents want educators to learn more about their home culture so that the teachers respect their children. This is accomplished by incorporating the community and family culture in the school curriculum. Including the family culture in the curriculum can take many forms. Essentially, the idea is for schools to make Latino parents and the community important companions in an ongoing dialogue.

Getting Latino parents involved in the school is only the first step in the program. How to maintain this involvement is equally important because parent involvement is not a one-time event. It is a continuous process that requires constant vigilance and adjustment to meet the needs of the school and the families. Parents can stay connected in many ways, but it is difficult to keep involvement active unless parent input is built into the daily curriculum and organization.

Making parents part of the curriculum means that they are co-teachers, as is the case in the bilingual preschool classroom illustrated below.

Elementary

CASE EXAMPLE

The teacher, Mrs. Terry Luna, trains parents to support her classroom curriculum. In her words, "I tell the parents that they own the schools. We work for them and they must understand as their children's most important teachers, they must stay interested every day in how their children are schooled." Mrs. Luna makes home visits to every family and communicates with them in Spanish. She enlists parents to assist her in the classroom on a daily basis. If they don't feel confident about being in the classroom, she convinces them that they are capable because, after all, they are teachers to their children every day.

Whatever abilities parents bring to the classroom when they volunteer, Mrs. Luna leaves nothing to chance. She systematically teaches the parents how to read to children, how to talk to children, how to instruct children in an art project, and how to understand the preschool curriculum.

Elementary

CASE EXAMPLE

Making Preschool Latino Parents Co-Teachers

Usually, all of the parents attend unless they have to work late on those evenings, and if that occurs more than once, I get on the phone and call their employer to make sure that they get out on time to attend the preschool meeting. I convince the parent and employer to have them make up the missed hours at another time. What I make sure of is that parents take their role as co-teachers seriously. Most of the time, they do. That's why I meet with them frequently. If I don't, they begin straying away, and then it's more difficult to get them back into a disciplined routine of working with their children at home and here in the classroom.

(Continued)

(Continued)

One thing that I have the parents do is to choose a committee of leaders that can organize their meetings and their agendas. That way, the parents decide what they want me to teach them and what they want to discuss at each meeting. The parents are wonderful leaders if we just step aside and let them make some decisions about their children's schooling. It certainly makes my work as a teacher easier to know that parents carry their share of responsibility for their child's education.

Almost on a weekly basis, Mrs. Luna holds parent meetings on Friday evenings, at which time she informs them about the preschool program, its curriculum, the children's progress, and ways to assist their children at home.

Elementary

SUGGESTION

To Keep Elementary Parents Involved . . .

- Communicate positive reports to parents about Latino students on a regular basis
- Motivate parents by paying attention to their personal life
- Support the family by referring them to local resources, and they will be more inclined to participate in the school
- Invite parents to visit the classroom for a special lesson
- Hold frequent focus groups for parents on informative topics of their choosing
- Have parents choose their own leaders to set their agenda at meetings

Keeping parents involved by training them to lead their own parent group makes these parents co-teachers with Mrs. Luna. Ongoing communication, in this case, happens as parents are taught to share with each other and assume responsibility for their children's education, not only in the home but also in the classroom. Mrs. Luna consistently stays connected with the parents by informing them about their children's progress and ensuring that they come into the classroom to assist when they are scheduled.

How educators and parents turn to each other as co-teachers takes many forms, but sustained two-way communication between educators and Latino parents is essential if all other facets of parent involvement are to succeed.

Despite high school students' wishes that their parents not show up at school or know about their doings on campus, it is equally important for high schools to maintain an ongoing dialogue with Latino parents. Approaches at the secondary level differ somewhat from those at the elementary level.

Just as educators expect parents to be co-teachers with them and to understand the school's curriculum, parents also want the school door opened to them with the welcome mat out.

Secondary

SUGGESTION

To Keep Secondary Parents Involved ...

- Communicate with parents positively about student progress
- Have students maintain a written log of homework for parents to review
- Remind parents to look at students' homework log
- Connect parents to community resources to support their family emotionally, psychologically, economically, and educationally
- Encourage parents to organize parent–advocacy groups with their own leadership and have those leaders co-lead school meetings

For Latino parents to stay involved, the school must create optimum conditions for communication to flow bilingually and continually. That begins before the parents even set foot on the school grounds.

Successful communication with Latino parents happens when interactions take place in a language of the home. A variety of verbal and written modes of contact are used to connect the school and the home. Messages to the home should be comprehensible to parents without being condescending. This way, students will perform better academically and socially. During all exchanges with Latino parents, educators need to consider sharing themselves, verbalizing feelings, articulating understandings, and discussing new possibilities.

SUMMARY

- There are many ways for educators and parents to communicate, through attitude, facial expressions, speaking, and writing.
- Students are important ambassadors when they deliver notes to parents from teachers and to teachers from parents.

- What makes communication effective is the willingness of both parents and educators to listen to each other, discuss, and negotiate a solution where one is needed.
- The most important thing for educators to remember is never to stop communicating with Latino parents.
- In communicating with Latino parents, teachers and educators develop a relationship of respect and trust.
- Educators who take the time to call, send notes, report positively about their students, and praise parental efforts to get involved receive stronger response from parents.

Agreement on issues between Latino parents and educators may not always be possible, but continuing frequent communication helps teachers and parents to share information on an ongoing basis. By so doing, they can keep the door open to unexplored possibilities.

4

Instructing Parents to Teach at Home

Latino parents value education and, to the extent that they are able, they support their children's schooling in many ways, limited only by their lack of knowledge of the school culture and its expectations. Home activities between Latino parents and children show what parents do to inspire their children, teach them language and literacy, and help them adjust to a different culture. Latino parents are the most important teachers for their children, and they may already know some ways to assist their children with their schoolwork. Educators can work along with parents to help them strengthen their own literacy as well as their parenting skills. Of assistance are parent education workshops to enhance the home activities that support children's education, including English as a second language for the parents, and to provide tips on doing homework with children and parenting skills; schools may also offer citizenship classes for parents (Delgado-Gaitan, 2001; Moles, 1993; Sleeter, 2001; U.S. Department of Education, 2001). Latino parents support their children's education by making their aspirations explicit, by joining them in literacy activities, and by helping children with homework activities.

CONNECTING

Parental Expectations for Latino Children

Family interactions in the afternoon and evening hours reveal the important role of parents as educators. Most activities revolve around the moment-to-moment business of maintaining a sense of family and accomplishing daily household tasks. Discussing school business is often woven in during meals, dishwashing, shopping, or doing laundry.

One way that parents motivate and encourage their children to excel and remain in school is through their own life experience. The spontaneous personal stories told across the kitchen table or en route to the doctor's office provide a view for children of their parents' experience of resilience, courage, value for education, and expectations for their success. The following story is an example. As parents sit with their 10th-grade son after he has brought home a letter from his teacher, the mother's sharing is instructive and firm, but still loving.

Secondary

PERSONAL VIGNETTE

Your teacher says that you have been clowning around in class when you should be working, especially during math. If you're having problems understanding math, then you should ask the teacher. You know that I don't like getting this kind of report from your teacher because it shows that you're wasting precious time. I get even more upset when I remember how impossible it was for me to get the education I wanted in Mexico. Your grandmother wanted me to go to school, but when I got to the second grade, my father died, and I had to drop out of school to help my mother at the *tortilleria* [a place where tortillas are made]. Every day I would wake up wishing that I could go to school instead of going to work. But year after year our family had more and more trouble making ends meet and eventually I gave up my dreams of going to school, but I vowed that when I had my own children, they would have all the opportunities that I didn't have to attend school. When your father and I immigrated to the United States, we made many sacrifices by coming to a place that we didn't know, learning a new language, and leaving our families behind so that we could have you attend better

---

schools here than we had in Mexico. It is even more disturbing for me to see that you're wasting your time when you should be studying because I know that you're very intelligent and capable of doing excellent work.

[Translated from Spanish]

NOTE: This Personal Vignette and others in this chapter are based on interviews, observations, and case files assembled by the author over the course of a 25-year career. In some cases, names have been changed to protect privacy, but any quotations are substantially the words of the original speaker, and the incidents occurred as described.

Teaching through personal experience connects parents and children to their family history while motivating the children to focus on their education. In most cases, the family's viewpoint coincides with the school's expectations. Even when the parents' academic experience is insufficient to assist their children directly, they make their expectations known.

School obstacles to Latino parent involvement include school culture, lack of parents' knowledge of school, and schools' ignorance of Latino family strengths and their inability to build on them. For Latino parents, staying involved in the schools means having educators that hold open the doors and reach out to the community in caring and effective ways. In the following example, the parent shares her experience of having her son's teacher act as an advocate for Latino families by holding monthly meetings with all of the parents of her fifth-grade students.

Elementary

CASE EXAMPLE

Mrs. Marin keeps us, the parents in her class, closely informed on everything that is happening in the classroom. She wants us to think of the classroom as our children's home. As parents we meet monthly to learn about what has been taught and to share what we think. Mrs. Marin also trains us to work with our children at home with their reading, writing, and math. She tells us that we need to

(Continued)

(Continued)

think of the kids' classroom as a home, and we are the family. Part of being in a family is to take responsibility for making it the best place possible. That means that we have to help our children at home. Reading is one area where my son, Carlos, needs a lot of help. But for many years, I thought that all I had to do was listen to him read. This past month, Mrs. Marin taught those of us who speak Spanish how to listen to our children read in English, and we ask questions in Spanish and they can respond in English because they're reading in English. It never occurred to me that I could ask my son in Spanish to tell me what he's read. Now, I feel more confident about working with Carlos on his schoolwork.

[Translated from Spanish]

NOTE: This Case Example and others in this chapter are based on interviews, observations, and case files assembled by the author over the course of a 25-year career. In some cases, names have been changed to protect privacy, but any quotations are substantially the words of the original speaker, and the incidents occurred as described.

What is taught and learned during these family events explains a large part of what Latinos consider important about their inner family relationship. In turn, those ties influence how children perform in school socially and academically. The following excerpt between Irene and middle-school daughter, Mary, exemplifies this.

Secondary

PERSONAL VIGNETTE

Late one Tuesday afternoon, Mary Segura, a middle-school student, came home from school. Her mother, Irene, was in the bedroom folding laundry. Immediately, Mary began complaining.

Mary: That teacher can't teach. He expects us to figure out how to work out that algebra, but he doesn't explain it.

Mother: I wish I could help you, dear, but that's beyond my understanding. You had a tutor at the school helping you. What happened with that?

Mary:	She's too busy, and she can only meet with me a couple times a week.
Mother:	Then let's figure out what more we can do.
Mary:	I've already tried. You need to go and get me out of that class.
Mother:	That's not the solution until I can see that you've done everything on your part.
Mary:	You can't expect me to get a good grade from that class with that teacher.
Mother:	It's not the grade that's as important as understanding the material. Let's find other people to help you.
Mary:	Who?
Mother:	Who in your class knows how to do these assignments?
Mary:	I know a couple of kids.
Mother:	Call them and set up a time and a place for you guys to work together. You can come here to study if you want.
Mary:	OK. I'll call them, but what if I don't get a good grade on this test?
Mother:	I'll go with you, and the three of us can talk about the problem after you've found every other avenue to get extra help.
Mary:	You're just taking his [the teacher's] side.
Mother:	I've already met with him, which is how you got the tutor on campus in the first place. Now you need to show me that you have a better attitude about doing more work on a subject that is difficult for you. I believe you when you say that you're having a difficult time, and your father and I want to support you in every way we can. But we also want you to want to learn. Some things are more difficult to learn than others. If just listening to the teacher isn't enough, then you need to find other ways to understand it.

(Continued)

(Continued)

Mary:	OK. I'll call my friends, but what if their parents won't let them come here?
Mother:	Then you go over there. You've got to believe that it is possible to learn this material, Mary. You sound as though you don't think it's possible to understand it. That's not the right attitude. You must think you're going to succeed.
Mary:	[takes a deep sigh and goes into her room, then comes out wearing a different outfit] I want to eat something. I'm going to need lots of energy to understand this stuff.
Mother:	By the way, yes, your father and I do expect you to get good grades. You just need to work differently and not use the fact that it's difficult as an excuse for not working harder.

In this interaction, Irene makes her expectations clear to Mary. Doing the best you can has some very specific expectations tied to it. For example, the Segura parents expect Mary to explore and exhaust the human resources around her that can assist her academically. Above all, however, Mary is asked to believe in her ability to learn and make every effort to succeed.

In spite of parents' inability to assist children directly in their academic homework, whether children are in elementary, middle school like Mary Segura, or high school, holding high aspirations and expectations for their achievement is a strong value in Latino households. Realistically, parents and educators need to have specific expectations for children, as did Mrs. Segura.

Elementary and Secondary

SUGGESTION

Parents and Educators Can Share Their Expectations for Students' Success by . . .

- Recognizing that all Latino children/students are capable of learning
- Holding children/youth accountable for completing homework by signing their homework sheet
- Expressing high expectations to children
- Exploring all avenues to ensure that students do the best work possible
- Helping children/students to change defeatist attitudes and believe in their potential

Elementary and secondary schools often provide homework contract sheets or homework binder sheets where students list the homework to be completed; parents are asked to sign after they review the work.

Homework is not an equal opportunity activity. Parents who have less experience with the school, have low academic attainment, or speak limited English find themselves even more isolated in a stressful situation than parents with more abundant resources. To break their isolation, Latino parents, teachers, and adolescents need to work together.

Latino parents have somewhat less difficulty completing homework with their elementary school children, but when parents do not understand the homework material, the problem remains.

Not all activity in the home is about schoolwork. In the down times, when schoolwork is put aside, a great deal of learning still occurs in the home. Latino parents believe that household activities are the platform for their children to

---

Secondary

SUGGESTION

Schools Can Break Parents' Isolation in Completing Homework by . . .

- Coordinating a public announcement with Spanish radio stations aimed at Latino parents to promote ways of doing homework
- Establishing a bilingual hotline number where Latino parents can get information on how to help their young people at home
- Working with parents, teachers, and students to develop individual contracts so that all three agree on homework responsibilities from the beginning of the school year and monitor them daily
- Opening a homework center that both bilingual teachers and parent volunteers can supervise, allowing students to complete homework with assistance
- Holding workshops for bilingual parents and students to learn how students can work in study groups with other students

---

succeed in the world. In some Latino families, parents may not be familiar with all the academic work that their children bring home, but they believe a caring home environment is very important. Many parents share this point of view and believe that such support has to begin at birth. The family's moral parameters are established then.

Elementary

SUGGESTION

Schools Can Help Parents in Getting Homework Done by . . .

- Holding bilingual parent focus groups at the beginning of the school year and asking Latino parents what would be the best way to stay connected with the school about homework completion
- Holding bilingual focus group meetings to hear from parents on their concerns about homework and the type of assistance that schools can offer
- Having parents call other parents to inform them of special workshops offered by the school to assist them in supporting their children's schoolwork
- Developing a "homework connection" handbook for parents to have as a reference for ways to help their children be accountable for completing homework
- Helping parents assemble a list of contact numbers where they can call for assistance when they cannot figure out how the work needs to be done
- Teaching parents that even adults with low literacy skills can hold their children accountable by having them explain the work that they completed
- Encouraging parents to organize informal support groups of parents to call each other when questions arise about homework
- Getting local high schools and colleges to assist elementary schools by providing them with tutors

Children need to be molded like clay to obey because, as parents often say, "they simply have to obey." Children show respect when they get older if they have been taught how to obey adults in their early years.

In Latino families, leisure time and social occasions often provide insight regarding family interactions and informal education. Family play, whether that means a Sunday soccer game or family celebrations, brings parents and children together to share language through stories and song.

Part of daily learning between parents and children occurs during emotionally packed moments that provoke confrontation, making negotiation an opportunity as this mother, Mrs. Dominguez, and her daughter, Rita, illustrate on the Sunday of the daughter's first communion.

The scenario shows a sensitive conversation between a mother and daughter. It appears that they had not previously communicated about Rita's likes and dislikes about her hair. Mrs. Dominguez listened to her daughter and considered her desires, then negotiated with her to reach an agreement that pleased them both. Through Mrs. Dominguez' use of negotiation and authority, Rita confided in her mother about her dislike of braids and her preference for a ponytail. Their ability to arrive at an agreement demonstrated how Latino families and parents use language to resolve problems.

Elementary

PERSONAL VIGNETTE

On that day, Rita wanted to fix her own hair, and her mother insisted on helping her because she wanted Rita's hair to look especially nice in braids. The tension built in the living room, and Rita went into the bathroom and locked the door. Her mother followed her and knocked on the door. From outside the door, the mother talked to Rita: "Dear, if you want to comb your hair, that's fine. I'll let you do it, but listen to me, this is not the way that you should behave, especially today. Come out and we can talk about it."

Rita opened the door, "I want a ponytail," she cried.

Her mother handed her a tissue, and she wiped her own eyes with another one, explaining to Rita, "Dear, today is a very special day for you, and I want you to look beautiful. Why are you so upset that I want to comb your hair?"

"No. It doesn't bother me that you want to comb my hair, but you always want to make me braids when I want a ponytail," complained Rita.

"I didn't know that you disliked braids so much. I'll make you a ponytail if you want." Rita continued to cry and her mother wiped her tears and they both went into the bathroom to comb her hair.

Latino parents view themselves as the most important motivators in their children's choice of career and desire for learning and succeeding. This Latino father, Mr. Alonzo, described his situation with his daughter:

If she is interested in pursuing a career, well all the better. Our interest is in our children and for their mind to assist their learning. If God wants them to have a career, well that's even better because at least they can defend themselves. Today there's so much [bad] that exists out there that one can't leave one's home. We want the best for our family, but sometimes it doesn't turn out like we plan.

A great many activities in the home help children learn about the world and their place in it, as this example illustrates.

Elementary

CASE EXAMPLE

Younger children in the elementary grades talk about their wishes for the future, while parents attempt to interject their own vision.

Marta sat on the couch giggling and talking with her mother, who had just arrived from working at a sewing factory. She told her mother that she knew what she wanted to do when she grew up. Her mother questioned her, and Marta replied that maybe she didn't know exactly the job. She sat and thought for a couple of minutes. Marta said that she liked flowers, and so a nursery would be fine as a place of employment. Her mother laughed and said, "Nursery?" Marta's mother told her that the most important thing was to think of a career, something useful, so that Marta would not have to work as hard as her mother has had to all her life. Marta then said that she would be a teacher. Her mother approved of her choice. She assured Marta that teachers also work hard, but she would not have to work from sunrise to sunset. Marta continued to fantasize about being a doctor who could work in a clinic so that she could help children and the elderly. Quickly, she added that perhaps she would like to be a policewoman like in the television series, "CHiPs." This sparked Marta's memory about the previous day's "CHiPs," and she began to relate the details of the episode. Her mother just sat and listened to her.

Parents use day-to-day events to socialize their children and teach them values about the importance of education and communicating with other members of the family. Parents support and shape career interests and family cohesion.

Career planning is not done formally when Latino parents do not have professional education. However, parents encourage their children to talk about their ideas and career plans in a casual way. In many homes, parents stress the many job possibilities and the type of schooling required for different careers. Older siblings talk to their parents about their desires once they finish high school. However, the reality is severe for those who do not achieve academically: They have few alternatives apart from going to junior college or working in agriculture, factories, or other short-term hourly employment. No matter how much Latino parents try to encourage and motivate their children in shaping their college and career directions, they may lack pertinent educational information that would help in deciding their children's future. That is a role that the schools need to assume systematically.

Schools can make a contribution to family interactions by conducting parenting workshops as part of a parent involvement effort. The parenting workshops that schools hold for Latino parents need to take into account how families interact in the home, how they use language, and how schools can strengthen family dynamics on issues of discipline, family stress, self-esteem, and communication with preadolescent children. In parent workshops, Latino community members and parents can relate to each other in their own language and share experiences common to Latino families. If Latino parents are co-teaching with educators, the parents taking the workshop will connect to the subject much more readily than if educators alone conduct the workshop.

> *Elementary and Secondary*
>
> # POINT
>
> ### Career Education and Higher Education Planning in Elementary Schools
>
> - Latino students need to begin thinking about college early in elementary school
> - Parents and educators need to create programs for children to explore college and career possibilities

SHARING INFORMATION

Literacy

Beyond emotional support, many parents guide their children to think about literacy. The types of reading materials that are found in the home vary depending on the magazines, *fotonovelas,* or books the parents prefer. Parents also pay attention to their children's educational activities by purchasing small storybooks, puzzles, and in some cases encyclopedias. When parents take their young children shopping, children may recognize the cartoon characters they've seen on book covers. For older siblings, buying books may be too costly, so parents encourage them to go to the library and check out the books they like. Parents also rely on children to bring home books from the school library.

Elementary

PERSONAL VIGNETTE

Six-year-old Raul wants his mother to read to him from one of his favorite books. He says he likes Little Red Riding Hood because he likes the part where the hunter kills the wolf and cuts it open to save the grandmother that the wolf has eaten.

Mother: You already know this story by heart.

Raul: No, no, no. I don't know it. I want you to read it to me. I like the wolf.

Mother: Once there was a little girl named Little Red Riding Hood. She was taking dinner to her grandmother. She was walking through the woods until she ran into a wolf. OOO eee OOO the boogie man.

The mother continued to hold the book and turn the pages. She stopped reading and told the story by just looking at illustrations.

Mother: Oh, see the wolf, he was very hungry. He followed Red Riding Hood. Look there he goes behind her.

Raul: He wanted to eat her.

Mother: No, no, he didn't want to eat her.

Raul: He wanted the tacos that she was taking to her grandmother.

> Mother: What do you think little Red Riding Hood did?
>
> Raul: She killed the wolf.
>
> Mother: [calling Raul's attention to the picture] But look at how little Red Riding Hood's grandmother ran and ran.
>
> Raul: She thought she could get away from the wolf.
>
> Mother: Yes, but then she tricked him, and what happened?
>
> Raul: I know. She called the police.
>
> Mother: How intelligent, my dear. Now you know what to do when a wolf chases you. Right?
>
> The child took the book and ran into his room, and the mother went into the kitchen to wash the dinner dishes.

Although reading favorite stories does take place in Latino homes, as students advance in grade level, leisure reading decreases in both languages. Parents feel less confident about the critical reading skills their children are learning, which increase in difficulty in the upper grades.

Where television is concerned, Spanish-speaking Latino adults favor Spanish programs, from the evening news to *novelas* (soap operas in Spanish). Many of the younger children also watch television with their parents, but as they become more proficient in English, they begin to request their favorite programs in English. Many parents prefer their children to watch TV in Spanish, especially the evening news, because they expect their children to maintain correct use of Spanish. Some Latino parents are more adamant than others about their children maintaining the Spanish language. Although parents understand that English is vital to their children's participation in society at large, they also want their children to preserve their native language.

Home literacy activities provide a framework for observing parents as educators in their natural social milieu. Literacy exists in Latino homes in forms ranging from emotional support for their children's desire to pursue schooling to storybook reading between parents and children. Young Latino children develop values about literacy through their interactions with adults in the home. Sometimes, the adults are the parents in the family, but they could also be members of their extended family: cousins, uncles, or aunts. In schools using English only, as students move up in grade, the reading material demands more of the parents. Parents may feel inadequate about reading with their children in English, but they try to stay engaged in their children's learning by encouraging them. This scenario with Jorge, a sixth-grade boy, and his parents illustrates the effort that Latino parents make to keep a hand in their children's schooling.

Elementary

PERSONAL VIGNETTE

Jorge is bilingual but prefers to speak in Spanish. His grades are mostly Bs and some As, but he is very bored. He claims to be going to school only because he knows the consequences would be even more painful at home if he were to drop out.

Jorge: I only have three days left of my summer school.

Mother: But that doesn't mean that you can run around.

Father: [smiling] You have to work.

Jorge: Work? I'm only in sixth grade, and I work really hard in school.

Mother: Well, while you're on vacation, you'll have to study something that interests you.

Jorge: I like art, and they won't let me into the class in the community center.

Mother: If you're really interested in art, then you have to go to the library and get books that you can read about art. When you're an artist, they'll look to you for opinions about art. And what are you going to tell them if you haven't read?

Father: Major artists like Frida Kahlo, Orozco, and Siquieros knew not only their own art but that of artists around the world. That's why they're famous.

Jorge: I don't like reading. I do it for school because I have to answer all of those questions at the end of chapters.

> Mother: But, dear, if you're interested in learning, you'll be able to read with patience and interest. Will you at least try?
>
> Jorge: OK, Mom. I'll try going to the library and checking out a book.
>
> Three weeks later Jorge revealed that he had been to the library and checked out a book on Mexican art and another one on Egyptian art. He told his parents,
>
>> I went to the library and got these two books, but I've only started reading the one on Mexican art. It's pretty interesting. It talks about Quetzalcoatl and other Aztec gods and how the Indians worshipped them. They used to sacrifice people to the different gods. I haven't gotten very far because my friends keep coming over, and they want me to be with them. So I don't know how long it'll take to read all those books. But what I really want is to be an artist, and I guess it's good to know all this stuff if I'm going to paint Mexican things.

Home literacy activities consume a good deal of time and effort for students and parents. Regardless of the type of reading materials that the parents prefer, some form of reading goes on in most Latino homes. Reading between parents and children happens most frequently before the age of eight, when there is ample opportunity for parents and children to interact around books and personal interests. Literacy values in a Latino family are shaped in context of the face-to-face communication between parents and children.

STAYING INVOLVED

Getting Latino parents to stay involved in their children's education and maintain connection with the school means that a well-defined structure needs to be in place for them to feel at home in the school.

In the ongoing process of parent involvement, Latino parents need to gain confidence about participating in schools. Learning what the family is about is the educators' role. Learning what the school is about and how it operates is the parents' role.

Homework Activities

For many Latino families, homework is much more of a problem than other parents face. The difficulties that Latino parents have in helping their children with homework have to do with the limits of their English proficiency and of their knowledge about the academic subject area in any homework assignment, as well as the lack of clarity of the assigned homework.

If students have academic problems in the classroom, they may actually spend more time doing homework than teachers believe. Parents, however, often spend a great deal of time with children who do not understand their homework. Children who are novice readers in the primary grades may spend 2 hours or more doing homework, with their parents alongside of them. The main problem is that parents do not understand what teachers expect any more than the children do. A familiar scenario looks much like the following one.

Elementary

CASE EXAMPLE

Just before dinner, Norma sat at the dinner table, and her mother stopped fixing dinner long enough to show her how to fill in the reading worksheet, which she had to complete. The exchange takes place in Spanish. Here it's translated into English.

Mother: Yes, dear, I'll help you right now. [Her mother sits down with Norma at the kitchen table and begins to work with her.] Let's see what you have to do.

Norma: What's a character?

Mother: [The mother continues to look at the book cover and points to illustrator's name and comments to Norma.] I think that this is the person you need.... Wait, this isn't it.

Norma watched as her mother looked at the book cover and found the book title with the name Zorro written in small letters at the bottom.

Mother: [She points to the book title.] This is the one who wrote the book.

Norma proceeds to write the book title in the space that called for the name of the author.

Like other parents in this group, this mother attempted to help her child with the homework question. She feels it is her responsibility to give her child the answers in order to get good reports from the teacher. This parent expresses a sentiment that is common among Latino parents. The reading worksheet is completed incorrectly, and Norma submits it to the teacher the next morning. The teacher then assumes that the child has filled out the sheet incorrectly because her parents are unable to assist her.

For Latino parents who have little or no experience with the formal school system, helping their children with their homework can feel like a major ordeal at the end of an exhausting day. Figuring out how to do it and when to do it, and then assuring that it's done correctly, can result in frustration and confusion. In parent education workshops, Latino families can learn to establish a regular, comfortable place in their home for doing homework and conduct frequent communication with the children's teacher(s) to clarify any misunderstandings about the assignment. As educators reach out to Latino parents to participate in

Elementary and Secondary

SUGGESTION

To Build Ongoing Partnerships . . .

- Have teachers teach Latino parents how to assist children in homework
- Let Latino parents co-teach "parent workshops" with teachers

Elementary

SUGGESTION

To Help Parents Help Children Get Homework Done . . .

- Attend meetings of an organized group of Latinos in the community—a migrant education group in the school district, church group, social group, or a civic group—that can reach parents
- Before workshops, have parents tell what homework concerns are
- Let teachers and parents co-lead workshops for parents and agree on a joint way to monitor students' work
- Pair up parents as buddies to network and support each other on a regular basis
- Organize a schoolwide hotline in Spanish that answers parents' questions

workshops led by school personnel, it's important to address those needs in a respectful way. Although Latino parents may believe that they need help in raising their children at home, it may be difficult for them to receive a communication from the school suggesting that they are "inadequate parents." Parents may resist educators telling them that they should "change their parenting ways" so that their children can succeed in school.

Above all, parents need to learn how to seek out resources to help their children with homework if it is something that is beyond their academic preparation.

The problem that homework presents for Latino students goes beyond the language difference. Some Latino parents who speak English and not Spanish still find homework a concern because of the amount of work that is assigned and the parents' limited educational experience. Embarrassment and shame often accompany this experience. Schools must get Latino parents to talk to them about what is difficult pertaining to homework and then provide parents with continuous workshops to train them on this subject. Community coordinators can reach out to Latino parents and begin and sustain the dialogue to get results: students doing their homework correctly.

Elementary and Secondary

SUGGESTION

Schools Can Provide a Supervised Space To Do Homework by . . .

- Opening homework centers on campus before and after school
- Providing a bilingual educator and volunteer at the centers
- Ensuring that parents know about the center and encourage students to attend

---

MENTORING PROJECT

Another method of tapping community resources to assist Latino students in their academic and social development is to organize a mentorship project in the schools. Professionals who work in the local community, as well as local college and university students, supply a wealth of resources as volunteer mentors for Latino students in the elementary and secondary grades. Schools and school districts have organized mentoring projects to supplement efforts on the part of individual schools and families to help the students. The suggestions that follow will help establish a mentorship project for Latino students.

Funding for a mentoring project can be obtained through local foundations and agencies that offer educators funds for literacy, parent involvement, and community organizing. In establishing a mentorship project, elementary and secondary schools need to learn about the Latino community, their language, activities, practices, beliefs, and values. To become knowledgeable about the community, educators can reach out to Latino parents and become familiar with ways that already work with their children. It is important to know what activities engage parents with their children/youth after school and on weekends and what kinds of expertise the parents possess. Identifying community leaders and learning about community centers in the neighborhood and activities they offer are also helpful. Knowing where parents take their children on weekends can help teachers to understand the students' social experience. Finding out where civic and social

> ### *Elementary and Secondary*
>
> # SUGGESTION
>
> ## To Get Mentorship Projects Going, Teachers and Administrators ...
>
> - Decide on how the mentorship project will operate—who will be involved, how parents will be contacted, how volunteer mentors will be screened, and what the academic activities are for them to emphasize
> - Write proposals to fund activities involving mentors and mentees, that is, field trips to universities, computers for class, necessary supplies, lunch, and so on
> - Decide on where and how often the mentors will meet the students—on campus, off campus, by phone
> - Have a community liaison or coordinator scout the community for businesses, universities, and other sources of volunteers

groups hold evening and weekend meetings in the neighborhood is helpful when planning school/family meetings. The social networks that parents belong to and the nonprofit agencies available to assist Latino families provide a landscape of resources that families can draw on for their daily needs. Teachers may also want to know what bilingual library services exist in the community as they plan classroom curriculum and homework assignments.

SUMMARY

Latino families and their behavior relative to supporting the children in their educational endeavors are enormously diverse. No one can judge from afar.

- The family is a system of interlacing communications.
- There's no right way to be a family, and Latino families strive to make it work.
- Latino families communicate and engage in literacy and home-work activities just as they do in family religious activities on Sunday and special occasions.
- Their day-in, day-out communication is reflective and constitutive.
- Their continuous interaction is constituted according to their social, cultural, and emotional environment.

5

Involving Families in the Life of the School

W hen they possess fewer of the educational skills required to participate in their children's schools in traditional ways, parents operate at a disadvantage. But as they learn to understand how the schools work, they can get involved. Instead of operating on the assumption that parental absence translates into not caring, educators need to focus on ways to draw parents into the schools. If we make explicit the multiple ways we value the language, culture, knowledge, and expertise of the parents in our communities, parents will participate more readily. Some teachers, principals, and counselors take walks around the neighborhood with school board members on weekends to become acquainted with the community where students live. Having guides such as school board members, and in some cases students and community leaders, and asking important questions makes educators more knowledgeable about ways to connect with Latino parents.

Educators need to use all available information in designing parent involvement programs in the school and districtwide. Schools are more likely to design meaningful activities when they work collaboratively with parents. In that way, Latino parents will participate in school activities and thus become more knowledgeable about supporting their children's/youth's academic progress.

Elementary and Secondary

SUGGESTION

Making Latino Parents Welcome Means That . . .

- Office staff and teachers speak the parents' language
- Educators and staff are nonjudgmental toward parents
- The school orients parents on finding their way around the school
- A parent center in the school has information on events and resources in Spanish for parents
- The school is used for community events that serve the Latino community

Latino Parents Need to Know . . .

- What does the school mean by parent involvement?
- What does the school expect from Latino parents?
- How does the school value Latino parents?

CONNECTING

As educators become informed about the community's social and cultural landscape, it becomes important to take stock of what the school district's definition of parent involvement is. What do educators mean when they say that they want parents to get involved in the school? Who decides what parent involvement means in a school district? Does it mean attending meetings, signing grade cards, tutoring in the classroom, signing off on funding proposals for the school, or attending English as a second language classes?

Schools need to make it clear to parents that their role in the school is important. The definition of parent involvement needs to be ample enough so that Latino parents can see themselves as important and capable agents in their children's education.

When they are unfamiliar with the school language, either because they are limited in English or because they do not know how to express themselves when they visit the school, Latino parents sense if school personnel are disapproving. Judgmental attitudes toward parents interfere in building a respectful relationship. In subtle ways, staff can convey messages of disapproval to Latino parents. If parents believe that the school disregards all of their efforts to assist their children and only takes notice of their attendance at parent-teacher associations and school site councils, Latino parents may potentially become discouraged.

Attendance—Those Present

Low parent attendance at school meetings need not be discouraging. In this society, we attribute a great deal of value to numbers, whether we are talking about student test scores or the low number of Latino parents who attend meetings in the school. However, the number of parents who attend a meeting is not always a true measure of potential interest. Often, although meetings and events show low attendance, much is happening. Gains have been made from previous parent outreach efforts; those present can make a difference and involve others. In spite of low attendance at meetings, teachers and parents may report more connection involving children's daily concerns in the classroom following any meeting where they can share information.

Elementary and Secondary

POINT

If Numbers Matter, Consider This

- Have I sent home reminders bilingually?
- Have I called parents?
- Have I asked a bilingual community member to contact the parents?

Latino parents participate in the schools in many ways, depending on the efforts that schools make to connect with the community. Whether parents attend school council meetings, visit the classroom to talk with the teacher, attend school assemblies, or work with their children on homework daily, they are involved in their children's education. What matters is that parents see themselves as critical, active agents in their children's education, both at home and in the school.

Parents as Spectators

When Latino parents show up at a school assembly and are rarely seen at other school events, they should not be dismissed as not caring about their children's schooling. They may be actively supporting their children in other less visible ways. Schools that want to engage parents in school activities need to view large, schoolwide events as an opportunity to attract Latino parents. Events such as assemblies and back to school nights are known to draw high numbers of Latino parents. Typically, when the children are involved in an assembly or some performance, parents are more inclined to attend. While it may be easy to believe that parents who are spectators are indifferent, the fact is that their presence indicates considerable interest. Such events provide an opportunity to invite parents to participate in the classroom in a particular way, to supervise on a field trip, or to help at a school workshop or fair. School-level activities are also opportunities to have Latino and non-Latino parents work together on events and issues pertaining to the entire school.

SHARING INFORMATION

In the early years of Latino children's education, much of parent involvement is almost invisible work. A primary activity for parents is coaching children to think about their strengths and to learn how to maneuver through the elementary and secondary school. A secondary aspect of parent involvement could socialize students to think forward beyond high school to attending college. Many Latino parents are unable to provide their children with basic information or assistance about attending college because they did not have the experience themselves. Thus, by getting involved in their children's education from the beginning of their elementary schooling, parents can learn how to socialize their children to the school's expectations, and this can prepare them for college.

Research has shown that parents are less helpful in preparing their children to think about college and professional careers if they have lower incomes and less education or are first-generation immigrants (Andrade, 1982; Lucas, Henze, & Donato, 1990). It is not that the less educated parents have lower aspirations for their children; rather, it is that their aspirations are less likely to be backed by informed resources and knowledge of how to work the school system. By the time that Latino students reach early adolescence, they are already at high risk of dropping out of school or of not being prepared academically to attend college; they may lose interest in school, fall behind scholastically, and drop out by their first year in high school.

The early work that educators have to do in socializing Latino students through school involves counseling children to do well academically with a vision beyond elementary and secondary school. To attend college, students must have taken all of the right courses in high school, and to get into those courses, students need to have taken the right advanced classes in math and English in middle school. Before that, to get good grades in algebra and English in middle school, students need to have a strong academic foundation in the elementary grades. Therefore, from their earliest years, Latino students need to have a strong academic preparation from educators and parents. Latino parents need to learn how to coach their children for college. Educators can help parents learn ways to start early socialization of their children in elementary school and through high school, ensuring that Latino students do not end their schooling when they graduate from high school. For example, in a workshop on planning for college that was held for parents of elementary school Latino children, a mother who assisted the director in the workshop shared her experience.

Secondary

PERSONAL VIGNETTE

I'm kind of lucky that I have an older daughter so I've had to get through all of the headaches of learning how to help her get the right classes so that she could apply for college. Then we had to beat the bushes for scholarships that she could apply for. Anyway, all of this information I would not have been able to have if it hadn't been for the program that Mrs. Casas directs. She taught us all the right questions to ask when we visit the school, teacher, and counselors.

It was difficult because my oldest daughter pushed me into the deep end with all the stuff about college, which I knew nothing about. But because I have a younger girl, she got to watch the entire process, and now she understands what she needs to do along the way. What I'm most glad about is that she recognizes the importance of doing well in school and preparing herself to apply for college and scholarships.

[Translated from Spanish]

NOTE: This Personal Vignette and others in this chapter are based on interviews, observations, and case files assembled by the author over the course of a 25-year career. In some cases, names have been changed to protect privacy, but any quotations are substantially the words of the original speaker, and the incidents occurred as described.

When educators invite Latino parent leaders to assist them in workshops for other parents, they can bridge the information gap between the school and the home. Teachers can provide Latino parents with information about the way the school culture functions;

parent leaders can share their first-hand experience of learning how to get their children successfully through the school system, with an eye toward college.

PARENTS AS ADVOCATES

First and foremost, the most powerful role that parents can exercise is to be advocates for their children in the schools. Youngsters in elementary and secondary school need to have an advocate on their side that they count on to believe in them through the good and the tough times. Some parents find their way through the complex school culture to deal with issues on behalf of their children regardless of obstacles. For Latino parents who are unfamiliar with the school system, advocating for their children can be like finding their way out of a maze. Yes, it's true that parents who speak limited English can walk on campus and demand to see the principal to settle a conflict involving their child. But we should not confuse what parents can do on a one-time basis with what is necessary for them to do as informed advocates over the long term of their children's schooling career. To be effective advocates, parents require information about how the school culture works. All educators can advocate for Latino students and families by reaching out to them, keeping them informed personally about their children, and teaching them how the school system works.

In a small suburban school district with about 45% Latino population, a Latino mother, Mrs. Guerra, describes how she always stays informed about and involved in what her children are doing in school. She recognizes that it is the parents' responsibility to stay informed about what their children do in school, and she complains fervently that the school diminishes the Spanish-speaking parents' role in their children's education.

Elementary

PERSONAL VIGNETTE

At home, my husband and I provide our three children as much as we can to encourage our children to do the best they can in school. We buy them books, and we take them to the library to check out others. They have strict hours for doing their homework. But more important, we emphasize that they should work hard at school and behave themselves. From the beginning of the school year, I go to meet my children's teachers. I tell them that they should call me anytime that I need to know about my children. I promise them that I will leave my work and be there as quickly as possible because I know that if the problem isn't resolved quickly, it only gets bigger.

For example, last year, my middle daughter who is now in the fifth grade was having lots of problems with a group of other girls who were picking on her. For a long time, the teacher did not tell me about the fact that she was spending lots of time in the principal's office. My daughter was afraid to tell me because she said that the other girls would beat her up. Finally, I learned about it from a neighbor who knows the girls who were picking on my daughter. I quickly went over to the school and demanded to see the teacher and the principal together. Although I don't speak English well, I make myself understood. My daughter had been wasting good learning time sitting in the principal's office, and this problem wasn't even her fault. She was the one being harassed.

This year, her teacher called me because she hadn't been turning in her homework. I left my work immediately, and when I arrived at the school, the teacher was surprised to see me arrive there so quickly. She said, "I barely hung up the phone." It works. It's not easy staying on top of it all with my kid's schools, but the alternative is even worse. My children deserve all the support they can get from us as well as from their teachers.

Even when the conflicts that require an advocate's attention are small, students need to know that they can count on someone to support them and hold them accountable for their behavior. Mrs. Guerra exemplified the role of advocate. Although some Latino parents are strong advocates in every way for their children's schooling, the schools also have a responsibility to communicate with parents systematically. Educators need to assist parents like Mrs. Guerra to advocate for their children by designing systematic ways to communicate with parents.

In the schools, many educators also play a strong advocate role. In this inner-city high school with a minority population of more than 70%, the counselor, Mrs. Byrd, is an active advocate for her students, as this 11th-grade Latina student, Angela, explains.

Secondary

PERSONAL VIGNETTE

Mrs. Byrd has been so helpful to me since I first came to this school as a freshman. Every time I need to change classes, she makes it possible for me to do and be able to get into more advanced college track classes. This entire school is tracked so that if kids are limited in English or if they don't get high scores in placement tests, they can't get into the advanced classes. But I've always gotten good grades in the advanced courses I've taken, and Mrs. Byrd recognizes that I work hard.

So every year I get placed in the low classes for students who are limited in English. Mrs. Byrd goes to bat for me and talks to the teachers and explains to them the problem. She tells them that I'm a good student and will work hard in their advanced placement classes, and I'm able to get into those courses that are required for college. She also calls me into her office to check and see how I'm doing. She lets me know if there is a contest or leadership classes or something that I can do after school to get involved in the community.

For Latino students, transitions between elementary and middle school and between middle and secondary school threaten their educational continuity. The complexity of the school system increases because they haven't had experience with formal schooling. This makes the advocate role in the school even more critical. The counselor in Angela's story illustrates the need for educators to be vigilant and address areas where many Latino students fall through the cracks if educators and parents fail to advocate for them. What typically occurs at transition points is that Latino students often miss crucial information about the coursework that follows them and the different expectations that await them. How to access and solicit the help that they need to maneuver through the educational system is the most important thing that students need to learn so as not to feel discouraged and leave school. Essentially, they need to learn how to advocate for themselves and to locate those who will shepherd and advocate for them. The role of advocates and educators is to guide Latino students through the transition from grade to grade by holding individual meetings with them to coach them on a regular basis.

HOME EXPERIENCES IN THE CLASSROOM

Teacher assumptions about the students' home environment can affect the relationship between home and school. Often, the assumption that "these kids don't live in literacy-rich environments" sets the home-school connection on an imbalance. Attempting to build a connection with Latino parents on this premise ignores the fruitful social inter-actions in the family. When educators fail to learn about Latino family activities, they may seem intrusive when talking with parents about ways to assist the children in their schooling. Latino parents may feel defensive if they believe that the teacher is attempting to tell them how to discipline children or how to help them to do homework in English when the teacher has not even asked them about their family. Latino parents offer a wealth of insights about their children's learning abili-ties and skills, which teachers can tap when they ask parents questions about the children's activities, likes, and dislikes, as well any home circumstances that may influence children's behavior in the classroom.

General questions about home activities and how parents might build on what happens in school are not useful to teachers because parents often don't understand that what happens in the home affects children's school performance. When teachers do not know what happens in Latino family life, they are inclined to believe that parents do not care about education, which in turn influences their attitudes about Latino student achievement. Latino parents complain about the low academic expec-tations that educators hold for Latino students. Unfounded expectations that students will not suc-ceed because their par-ents are dismissive about their children's schooling and will not hold educa-tors accountable are far too common (Finders & Lewis, 1994; Jones, 2002). Therefore, parents and teachers need to share high expectations so that they have a mutual purpose for the students' academic achievement.

> *Elementary and Secondary*
>
> ## POINT
>
> ### Holding High Expectations for Latino Students ...
>
> - Is a critical belief that supports learning
> - Is a common goal that can be shared by both parents and educators

Teachers can learn from parents about their expectations for their children. When teachers ask specific questions about how parents talk

Elementary and Secondary

SUGGESTION

Some Questions to Ask to Learn About the Latino Community, Its Language, Activities, Practices, Beliefs, and Values

- What activities engage parents with their children/youth after school and on weekends?
- What expertise do adults possess?
- Who are the community leaders?
- Are there community centers in the neighborhood, and what activities are offered?
- Where do parents take their children on weekends?
- Where do groups hold evening and weekend meetings in the neighborhood?
- What social networks do parents belong to?
- What nonprofit agencies are available to assist Latino families?
- What bilingual library services exist in the community?

and read to children, they gain insights that can strengthen the classroom program. Specific questions can ask how parents and children spend time together, the type of reading they do together, the type of writing that the family engages in, and the favorite topics of conversation among parents and children.

When teachers learn about family interests and activities, they have an advantage when making recommendations to parents about ways to build continuity between school and home activities. For example, when teachers inquire about the type of reading that parents do with children, they sometimes learn that reading the Bible is a regular literacy activity in Latino homes. Although religious texts are not read in the school, some connection can be made. This teacher feels that knowing what the parents share about their literacy practices at home can inform her third-grade classroom.

Elementary

CASE EXAMPLE

I was aware that some of my students belonged to the local Catholic Church, but I didn't have a clue how much Bible reading they did at home. Apparently, it's a practice in this church that I didn't know about. One parent told me about it when I asked her how much reading her daughter, Monica, did at home. She began telling me about the lessons that her daughter had to do for their religious training classes. I was impressed and took that as a clue to make sure that I build more into the reading lessons on the kinds of areas that many of these students find in their Bible reading. I can do it with history, folklore, and myths.

NOTE: This Case Example and others in this chapter are based on interviews, observations, and case files assembled by the author over the course of a 25-year career. In some cases, names have been changed to protect privacy, but any quotations are substantially the words of the original speaker, and the incidents occurred as described.

In secondary schools, parents, youth, and teachers have a different agreement about the way in which parents get involved. Where Latino students are concerned, parents want to stay involved and to learn as much as possible about the possibilities for their children's future. Unfortunately, as early as middle school, many Latino students drop their academic courses, which has devastating academic consequences in high school if not handled adequately in the middle school. During these school years, parental involvement is critical, as the academic future of Latino students hangs in the balance (Jones & Vélez, 1997). The question is, how can schools get parents involved in a meaningful way and keep them informed

Secondary

SUGGESTION

To Build Partnerships Between Middle and High Schools and Latino Parents . . .

- Teachers need to stay informed about the home life of Latino students and how it may be impacting the students' academic performance; talking with the students and becoming aware of their situation assists the school in designing an intervention plan to meet their academic needs.
- Academic plans for Latino students must always include the parents' perspective as well as that of the respective educators.

(Continued)

(Continued)

- An individualized learning plan needs to be designed for Latino students who are performing below grade level.
- A bilingual dean, teacher, or teacher assistant needs to communicate with the parents of the student involved by phone.
- Parents should be asked to bring someone with them whom they trust or who can interpret for them—such as a family member, minister, or social worker—if the school does not have a bilingual translator.
- Conferences to design an individualized academic plan for students in academic peril need to include the student and the parents as well as the educators.
- Latino parents need to be informed of the resources available to them to help them in supporting their youth, for example, homework centers, tutors, psychological counseling, or medical services.
- On a weekly basis, a bilingual person needs to contact the parents to monitor the parent's role in executing the individualized academic plan.
- Finally, middle and high schools need to provide workshops for Latino parents to help them understand how they can support their young people through this period in school.

about student academic progress?

Since the purpose of parent involvement is fundamentally to ensure student academic success, getting middle and high school parents engaged in the planning of students' academic expectations is necessary. When parents are involved in the discussion of academic plans for Latino students, they can help guide the student's work at home, even if they themselves cannot directly assist them in the subject matter. Middle and high schools need to provide workshops for Latino parents to help them understand what they need to do to support youth in this age group to succeed in school.

PARENT VOLUNTEERS IN THE SCHOOL

Latino parents are visible as volunteers in offices, playgrounds, or cafeterias and on the streets that surround the school, enforcing discipline and caring for students in places where school personnel cannot be at all times. Although many schools believe being a school volunteer is not a popular role for Latino parent involvement, many middle-size schools have successfully involved Latino parents as volunteers. A way of getting Latino parents to volunteer is by organizing a group of parents to identify other interested parents. In the suggestion box below, there are steps that schools have taken to convene a group of Latino parents in a school. This is often more successful if a community liaison is part of the school personnel. Where a community coordinator is not available, principals step in to meet with Latino parents on a weekly basis by holding a mid-morning coffee time to talk.

Teacher use of the home culture in classroom instruction and curriculum is an important way of sharing information about the Latino family culture. One teacher describes how she uses the home language, values, and culture to enrich the classroom curriculum.

Elementary

SUGGESTION

To Recruit Latino Parents as School Volunteers . . .

- Have each teacher suggest one or two parent leaders who are involved or show interest through their presence at school (made known through questions they have posed to teachers and other school personnel)
- Hold regular meetings of this Latino parent group with a principal, community coordinator, or resource teacher to make decisions on issues pertaining to Latino students and their families, for example, communication with Latino families by phone and through school newsletters, discipline, testing, curriculum, or special placement
- Make meetings short, informative, and pertinent to the business of children's learning
- Use the Latino parent group to identify other parents who can get involved in school events

Elementary

CASE EXAMPLE

Ms. Vega describes her third-grade classroom:

It is very important to incorporate the home culture in the curriculum so that the parents and students feel good about who

(Continued)

(Continued)

they are, where they come from, where their fellow students come from, and feel good about the language they speak. We honor students as star of the day and star of the week, spotlighting books, songs, poems, and artwork from the children's cultures as well as from others. We also openly talk about issues that are happening at home, both the positive and negative ones. Respect for all cultures is a general theme in all areas of learning. If children learn to see the good in all people, they will most likely see it in themselves, and the parents will feel like they belong in the classroom, too. That way the classroom is also a familiar place for parents when they visit. Some of them even offer to do some activities with the students on things like music or building birdhouses.

Elementary and Secondary

SUGGESTION

To Use Community Resources...

- Develop a trusting relationship with parents so that they know that you mean what you say about having them in the school
- Maximize community expertise—parents have talents, which teachers can use
- Start parents thinking about talking to their children about high school and college and careers

This teacher has found a way to bring the students' culture into the classroom, and in so doing, she made parents feel comfortable enough to become a resource in the classroom. There are numerous ways for teachers to familiarize themselves with the talents in the community and to integrate them in the classroom curriculum.

STAYING INVOLVED

Parents as Classroom Volunteers

Volunteering in the classroom is an important way for Latino parents to contribute to their children's schooling and to learn about the school system. Not only do teachers need a great deal of assistance in the classroom to offer an activity-rich curriculum, but volunteering is an opportunity for parents to observe how the school functions. Parents possess a wealth of talents, and teachers, community liaisons, and principals are quite resourceful in discovering the myriad skills available in the pool of Latino parents in every classroom. Matching up the parents' skills with the classroom's needs is a teacher's prerogative in accordance with the classroom curriculum plan. Some ways to tap into Latino parents' talents, expertise, and interests is to identify the music, culinary, and gardening experts; tutors in subject areas; storytellers; computer whizzes; and people with good supervisory skills or any other talents. Classroom parents and community leaders can be recruited to help in these ways. The ideal, of course, is to have the parents present in the classroom, but some parents find that time is a barrier to volunteering in the classroom. However, there are ways to tap into their talents, which they can share even if they cannot be present. Parents can share their expertise through their children, who can bring stories, food and recipes, or musical instruments, which represent the parents' gifts.

Integrating Latino culture into the classroom through parent volunteers plays a dual role. Students can appreciate that Latinos are capable in a variety of expert areas, while parents can view themselves as an integral part of their children's classroom experience. Making the volunteer experience a productive and successful one for everyone involved requires that teachers or other educators train Latino parent volunteers. The important thing to consider when involving Latino parents as volunteers is that they should participate throughout the school year. Latino parents have much more than a Cinco de Mayo cooking

Elementary

SUGGESTION

Integrate Latino Culture in the Classroom Through . . .

- Storytelling
- Tutoring in language
- Using regional music instruments and song
- Reading poetry or literature from Latino countries
- Studying a Latino country
- Learning dances of a specific region
- Mapping geography of Latino countries

recipe or dance demonstration to offer. They should share their music or culinary skills throughout the school year. The point is to provide a well-rounded representation of the Latino experience.

Secondary

SUGGESTION

Integrate Latino Culture in the Curriculum Through...

- Reading literature by Latinos in the United States
- Studying the history of Latinos in the United States
- Taking Spanish language instruction
- Learning the geography of Latino countries and U.S. demographics

Parents as Decision Makers

Parents are important decision makers throughout their children's career in school. Much of the parental influence takes place in the home. However, schools have formal avenues in which parents can participate. Issues of budget, curriculum, and other school policies are considered. Not all Latino parents can be expected to serve on school committees; some may prefer to get involved in other ways. Some cannot attend meetings if they are held during their work hours or if the school is a long distance from their home. Educators can adjust time and distance to accommodate parents. Meetings can be held during hours when most parents can attend, and they can also be held at community centers closer to their neighborhoods. But serving on school committees also requires parents to be knowledgeable about how the school operates. Other skills for decision making on school committees involve the ability to do long-range planning and to have a wide overview of all of the school's programs. Collaboration between teachers and parents is a critical aspect of decision making.

Elementary

POINT

Typical Skills Required in Decision Making in Schools

- Understand how school programs and curriculum operate
- Understand how the rules of order operate in meetings
- Understand short- and long–term goal setting in schools
- Understand how to represent Latino families and community interests

If Latino parents are to participate effectively, they need to have some training on how to serve on committees. The school's administration, with the assistance of Latino parent leaders, needs to conduct workshops for parents to teach them how to serve on committees. In one case, a county administrator and parent leaders hold meetings for Spanish-speaking Latino parents to participate as decision makers in the high schools.

Secondary

CASE EXAMPLE

Mrs. Sanchez contacted Latino parents who have been active on school committees and asked them to participate in a program. The parent leaders spoke to the audience of other parents:

> As Spanish–speaking parents, we can share our experience in getting involved in the school. It's important that you get involved in making decisions on committees because [these affect] books, curriculum, and matters in the classroom. Our children's schooling is decided by some of the school committees. Speaking Spanish should not stop you from sharing your ideas with other parents and school personnel.

> Some of the questions that Latino parents asked were

> - How do we know what is right for the school to do?
> - Is it right for us to make decisions when we don't understand the issue?

> Parent leaders and the county coordinator instructed the Latino parents to talk with other parents about the issues that have to be decided.

> You also need to ask questions at the meeting if you do not understand everything that is involved. Don't be afraid because you don't know. Ask questions when you're in the meeting, but also talk to other parents whom you know. You become more informed when you take a risk and ask questions.

Parent leaders shared their personal stories on how to get involved in the school. One person synthesized a way that parents can overcome fear and begin expressing their voice in school committees. In the case example below, Mrs. Lopez, the parent leader, relates how collective energy on the part of parents helped her to advocate with the school on behalf of her third-grade son.

Elementary

CASE EXAMPLE

For a long time, I couldn't understand how it was possible or even necessary for me to get involved in committees where they talked about the school curriculum or budget. It all sounded boring and impossible for me to understand. No one I knew ever attended these meetings.

Then when my son got into third grade, his teacher told me that she thought he should be in a gifted program but that the school did not accept bilingual students in the gifted program. The teacher said that she didn't make the decisions about admitting students into the gifted program but that I could talk with the principal about it. That bothered me so much that I told my husband that he had to go with me so I could talk with the principal about it. I needed support and courage!

We both went and I spoke very broken English. The principal asked me if I needed someone to interpret. I told him I would try to say as much as I could, and he listened carefully. My husband knows a few more English words, but he was quiet most of the time. I explained that I wanted my son in the gifted program, and I felt that just because he was limited in English he shouldn't be excluded from the gifted program.

The principal explained that there was a school policy that had been set by the committee that works with special programs. I had no idea what that meant, and I told him that he should change it. He explained that he couldn't, only the committee could change it. He said I had to go and explain to them what I had told him.

That still made no sense to me, but I was in high gear and the committee was my next stop. The principal told me when they met and that I could attend and listen and express my concern. There were a couple of other parents there, but they had other concerns. The teachers in the committee listened to my concern, and they agreed to examine the situation with the gifted–student criteria for admission into the program.

A few weeks passed, and I didn't hear from them. So my husband and I went back to meet with the principal. He said that examining the program criteria would take much longer than a few weeks.... Then he suggested that if I wanted to, I should get other parents who have had a similar problem to come with us to the committee the next time it met. Now I was determined to see that my son's situation got resolved. I decided to ask my son's teacher about other children in the same situation.... There was only one other in my son's class, but she knew of others. So there I began knocking on my neighbors' doors. I convinced them to attend the next meeting at the school.

The changes that happened in getting bilingual children accepted into the gifted and talented program took months. But they began in the committee with all of us parents and teachers talking about the problem. If I hadn't gone through it, I wouldn't have believed that it was possible to learn so much about the school and help to make some changes by serving on this committee. I'm so glad that I got angry enough to go into that principal's office to ask questions about getting my son into the program.

The outcome of those months of working with the teacher committee was that this parent leader was invited to be a parent representative on the committee. Over the years, she not only got involved, she was instrumental in getting other Latino parents involved in committees to speak up for Latino students' rights.

It is possible for Latino parents who do not have a long tradition of working on committees to find an entry point into the governing life of the school. Administrators and teachers educate parents by coaching them on how to navigate the bureaucratic conventions of elementary and secondary schools.

Elementary and Secondary

SUGGESTION

For Latino Parents to Participate in School Committees, Schools Need to . . .

- Provide translation for parents who are limited English speakers
- Use jargon-free language in the meetings
- Listen to parents' perspective
- Include parents' perspective in decisions

How decisions are made in different school settings differs minimally. In most cases, committee meetings are open for parents to attend. Schools can encourage Latino parents to participate in committees as decision makers by holding meetings bilingually. That is, translation does not have to be simultaneous, but meetings can be conducted so that a concept or a point is made in English, then translated into Spanish. What parents do expect is equity: They must receive all of the information in Spanish that is delivered to English speakers in English. Interaction among committee members also needs to be translated so that everyone participates in the discussion. The reverse is also necessary. When Spanish-speaking parents speak, their comments need into be translated to English for others (Shannon, 1996).

All schools and all levels of schooling have some form of parent group. Whether it's a parent-teacher organization or school site council, there is a time when educators and parents meet to deal with their respective agendas. In the case of the parent-teacher association or organization, the purpose is typically fundraising for the school, while councils deal with policy, budget, and school program issues. Regardless of the group's purpose, the leader has the power to influence how inclusive the group is. When a Latino(a) is in a leadership position, the group seems to attract more Latino participation. The message is, never underestimate the power of one. A single person brought into a group can be a catalyst for others. One does make a difference.

Parents as School Employees

Schools that hire community members to serve as assistants and supervisors build a stronger connection with the community. When schools hire bilingual-bicultural teaching assistants from the community for the classrooms, they give them an opportunity for employment as well as validating the community language, cultural, and skill pool. Latino children get to see familiar faces and hear familiar language in school employees, which builds self-esteem.

From that same pool of community members, schools often hire paid supervisors for playground and lunchroom duty. Latino community liaisons are also important paraprofessionals in schools, linking the Spanish-speaking families with the school. When liaisons are members of that community, parents develop a strong trust and are apt to respond better to the school's invitation to get involved.

Teacher assistants, community liaisons, and library assistants, as well as playground and lunchroom supervisors, need to receive training from school personnel. Although they speak the language of the community and are familiar with resources that benefit families, they need to understand the importance of confidentiality when working with families.

Another way of involving Latino community talent and skills in the elementary classroom is in the capacity of workshop co-leaders. When training teachers during teacher preservice and inservice workshops, Latino parent leaders can assist teachers as co-leaders. As co-leaders in workshops, they can supply information about the culture and the community that teachers can use to relate better to students and their parents.

Elementary and Secondary

POINT

Requirements of Partnerships Between Parents and Educators

- Educators learning from the community
- Consulting Latino community leaders in teacher preparation programs
- Employing Latino parents to co-teach other teachers in workshops

---

SUMMARY

- Educators play a critical role in the success of the parent involvement process.
- When school administrators, community liaisons, and teachers take clear and deliberate steps to involve Latino parents in the classroom, in advisory committees, and in school activities, the border that divides Latinos and the schools blurs. Students, parents, and educators win, as they work together to improve student achievement.

6

Preparing Latino Students for Higher Education

T he long journey to college begins in the elementary school years and steadily gains importance through high school. Schools as well as parents play a central role in socializing students to college. There is a significant difference between students who just "get by" in school—they may graduate from high school but not attend college—and students who "get ahead." Students who just "get by" tend to come from families that may be poor: Parents may want their children to succeed in school but lack the knowledge to access the educational resources to support their children. Students who "get ahead" tend to come from families who continuously stress high grades, are involved in school activities, and discuss options for colleges and careers. The key difference is the know-how, which some parents possess more than others. It's the know-how that Latino parents gain through participation that develops parent potential and skills (González, 1995).

The Mother/Daughter program described in this chapter is premised on the idea that getting Latina girls to graduate from high school and to enter college requires a systematic partnership between the school, the family, and the university. The Mother/Daughter program is a successful model of a partnership between schools, school districts, Latino families, and local universities in the four states (Arizona, California, New Mexico, and Texas) where it operates (Tomatzky, Cutler, & Lee, 1990a, 1990b).

The Mother/Daughter program is highlighted as a model for educators to consider designing and implementing in their schools. The Mother/Daughter model as a project has been successful, and it provides an excellent template for schools. Although the features of the program focus on serving only girls, there is a critical need for such a program to serve boys as well as girls. Therefore, in the Point and Suggestion boxes, I extend the principles of the program to include male and female Latino students.

Elementary and Secondary

POINT

To Latino Parents, *Know-How* Means . . .

- Understanding school requirements
- Learning to access resources
- Sustaining advocacy for students throughout their schooling

CONNECTING

Using the knowledge of educational development and an understanding of traditional Latino family dynamics as a guide, the Mother/Daughter (MD) program is built around three innovative elements: (a) educate mothers and daughters about getting the girls to college, (b) provide the daughters with academic support toward that end, and (c) socialize the mother/daughter teams to the college through field trip experience. Educational research and life experience have taught us that mothers exert a powerful influence on their children's decision making. This influence is even greater in the traditional Latino family. Latino girls in traditional families are often not encouraged to pursue higher education because parents have heard that it is costly. Thus, just getting through high school is sometimes the best they think they can do (Andrade, 1982; Asher, 1984; Delgado-Gaitan, 1994b; Flemming, 1982; González, 1995; Johnston, Markle, & Harshbarger, 1986). The problem is that these young people are relegated to low-income employment thereafter.

Underemployment and low educational attainment in the Latino community remain high because many Latino students fail to attend college. Latinas fare even worse than Latino men. About 71% of Latina girls in some school districts do not graduate from high school. However, rather than focusing solely on the dangers of dropping out of high school, the Mother/Daughter program is a proactive and constructive effort that focuses primarily on the vast challenges and rewards of academic achievement, of attending college, and of establishing a professional career. For that reason, the Mother/Daughter program is successful.

Evidence of the success of the MD program is shown by the outcomes for first-year participants in Texas, who were high school juniors at the time of the study. The girls began the program in the fifth grade.

- 98% of the girls were still enrolled in school.
- 62% of the girls were enrolled in advanced college-prep classes.
- 27% of the girls were enrolled in honors classes.
- 76% of the first-year and 62% of the second-year girls were A or B students.

The Mother/Daughter program has been operating since 1985. The program began in El Paso, Texas, and was subsequently adopted by school districts in Tempe, Arizona; Albuquerque, New Mexico; and San Mateo, California. The programs vary by number of participants, duration of program, and specific activities. However, the major goals and general practices are common to all of the Mother/Daughter programs in the four states where it operates. It can be replicated and adapted to include Latino males as well as females and fathers as well as mothers.

The Mother/Daughter program begins with the recruitment of girls in

---

Elementary and Secondary

SUGGESTION

To Initiate a Latino Parent/Student Program . . .

- Designate a coordinator to function as an administrator to obtain funds, coordinate teachers and tutors, meet with parents, and deal with colleges
- Obtain funding from federal agencies, foundations, local agencies, and the school district
- Designate a teacher to work with students in academic tutoring at school and conduct classes for them on study skills

the spring. Teachers often submit names of girls who would make good candidates for the program.

Although most of the girls selected for the program have academic achievement difficulties, one of the programs does admit girls who have high academic promise, along with those whose academic performance is below grade level.

> *Elementary and Secondary*
>
> ## SUGGESTION
>
> ### Criteria for Selecting Latino(a) Students For a College-Bound Program
>
> - Families with low income
> - Parents with low educational attainment
> - Students in academic peril

Four programs begin in the elementary grade levels, and add one grade level each subsequent year. The Mother/Daughter program continues through high school. It is designed to encourage parental commitment to higher education and helps Latina girls to make choices about their future by familiarizing them with academic options. To qualify for the program, students must be first-generation college candidates and demonstrate academic promise in school. The program provides ongoing counseling and mentoring through high school and college. Girls are encouraged and supported academically to complete high school and apply for college. In addition to tutoring and mentoring, the Mother/Daughter program offers the girls university tours, field trips, and community service opportunities. For the mothers, the goal is to teach them how to be good parents and role models.

In families where mothers and fathers are present, both parents can benefit from this type of college orientation, and their sons as well as their daughters can take advantage of parent and student training in the program.

Mother/Daughter Program Activities

The proposed MD program consists of activities designed to help girls and their mothers enhance their interest in school and raise their educational and career aspirations. Mothers are a central focus of the program because their expectations, their involvement, and their role modeling have a lasting impact on their daughters' educational development and career choices.

Change in one family member means change in the family dynamic. The extended effect of the program benefits other family members. Mothers like Mrs. Segura tell how their husbands and younger children have benefited from their participation in the Mother/Daughter program.

Elementary and Secondary

PERSONAL VIGNETTE

Before I began participating in the Mother/Daughter program, my husband wouldn't let me leave the house for anything having to do with the schools or anything social. I had about 10 years of schooling in Mexico before leaving there, but then I got here and got married and had my two daughters, and there never seemed to be enough time to get an education here. So when our children began school and the teachers used to send notices about meetings, my husband wouldn't let me attend. He said that it wasn't important and that it was a waste of my time. I wanted to go just to see what it was all about, but I was afraid to go by myself since I didn't know anyone. Then my girls got older and fortunately they were good students.

Then when the youngest daughter, Monica, was in the fifth grade, I received a notice that she was being selected to participate in the Mother/Daughter program. It sounded so interesting, and I lied to my husband the first few times that I went to the Saturday meetings to meet with other moms and the director. Well, finally, I got the nerve to tell him where I was really going on Saturdays. He still said it was a waste of time but he didn't object to my attending. By now I had convinced him that it was very important that I be there to learn as much as possible about ways to help Monica. By then, he had noticed that this daughter needed more direction and support than our oldest daughter, who was very disciplined. I think that's why he didn't object as much. And as the program continued and Monica entered middle school, I learned more and more at the Mother/Daughter program. I learned how to discipline her at home and how to advise her to do her schoolwork and how to seek the help she needed in middle school, both academically and in her social adjustment.

Now that she's in high school, her challenges are many, but if I wasn't involved in the Mother/Daughter Saturday group with other

Latina mothers, learning how to advocate for her, she wouldn't be doing as well as she's doing. My husband does not say anything against me attending meetings or school functions anymore. Although he doesn't attend with me, he has seen the positive results with both of our daughters. And his way of supporting is by remaining quiet.

[Translated from Spanish]

NOTE: This Personal Vignette and others in this chapter are based on interviews, observations, and case files assembled by the author over the course of a 25-year career. In some cases, names have been changed to protect privacy, but any quotations are substantially the words of the original speaker, and the incidents occurred as described.

Mrs. Segura, like other mothers, learned that the family dynamics in the home change as one person grows. In Latino families, the ties are strong, and the woman's role holds a great deal of authority in reference to children's schooling. Men commonly relegate the responsibility to women, so in the absence of school programs like the Mother/Daughter program, Latina women miss out on social networks with other women and school personnel where they can obtain critical knowledge.

SHARING INFORMATION

The knowledge shared collectively among participants in the Mother/Daughter program empowers the mother and daughter participants. School personnel recognize the fruits of their work as Latino parents become informed. As a consequence, Latino students also become better informed and more interested in their schooling, and they become independent learners.

School/School District and Community Role

Activities take place in three major areas: the school, school district, and the community at large, including the university campus. The girls and their mothers participate in activities planned by the school district, which take place at the schools and at various sites in the community. School activities focus on developing the girls' academic readiness by introducing them to computers. Through

> **Elementary and Secondary**
>
> ## SUGGESTION
>
> ### Beginning in the Fifth Grade and Continuing Through High School, These Activities Support a Latino Student's Goal to Attend College
>
> - *Tutoring.* Students receive regular academic tutoring from college student volunteers
> - *Mentoring.* Students are paired with local professionals to assist them
> - *Study skills classes.* Students are taught how to budget time, obtain resources, and discipline themselves
> - *Computers classes.* Both students and parents receive instruction
> - *Volunteering in the community.* Students perform service projects in the community
> - *Personal identity presentations.* Students attend workshops with counselors to discuss and write about their identity

presentations, schools help the girls and their mothers to focus on their personal identity as individuals, members of Latino families, and members of American society. As elementary and secondary schools consider designing a project of this type to include both boys and girls, some practical suggestions are listed in the box.

Community activities introduce the participants to the many resources around them. The girls and their mothers visit various community sites, including the medical center, city hall, historic missions, the public library, and the museum of art. They attend a symphony or theater performance or participate in a health fair for women taking place in the community.

Each of these experiences broadens the participants' development as individuals and community members and as future leaders within their community.

The Parental Involvement Component

Parents participate in well-designed activities to acquire the necessary skills and expertise to exercise parental commitment to their children's education. The Mother/Daughter program organizes activities for the girls and their mothers around four broad themes: (a) building girls' self-esteem, (b) orienting the girls to higher education and professional careers, (c) improving the quality of preparation for higher education, and (d) increasing Latino parental commitment. The program activities are designed for mothers to become acquainted with careers involving higher education, especially nontraditional careers for women in math and science.

Increasing the involvement of Latina mothers takes on a special literacy-related meaning in the California project. The mothers participate in a personal literacy activity that the director, Dr. Carmen Contreras, calls Mother Stories.

Mothers' Stories Literacy Activities are held monthly for twelve months. The girls' mothers meet as a group to discuss topics related to mother-daughter relationships. The literacy process is a three-hour session in four parts: (a) reflecting about a specific topic, (b) writing, (c) reading their written text to the group, and (d) sharing and discussing. The collective aspect of this process provides mutual support to the women and creates a safe environment for those women to think and express themselves. The process is intended to break the cycle of isolation for these mothers who may feel distant from others when raising their daughters. Isolation typically breeds fear, intimidation, and nonparticipation. Engagement allows adults to connect with their own history, culture, and family and with others in their community, enabling them to feel more empowered. Initially, specific topics are selected for the mothers, but as the project moves along, the participants are asked to suggest topics relevant to their particular experience.

> ### *Elementary and Secondary*
>
> # SUGGESTION
>
> ## Invite Latino Parents to Discuss, Write, and Share Their Personal Stories About...
>
> - Recalling important parts of their own childhood relative to school
> - Identifying values they most want to impress on their children
> - Developing their own confidence socially and academically
> - Influencing their children's peer groups
> - Finding their children's life interest
> - Spending time with their children
> - Disciplining and setting limits for their children

Mothers meet in a local community center and library on Saturdays for two hours with the project coordinator to discuss, write, and share their personal stories.

Each literacy assignment is designed to have the mothers express their own childhood experience on the topic and their efforts to deal with their own role as mothers. In the literacy activities, mothers increase their awareness of issues and values about which they need to speak with their daughters as they guide their daughters through schooling. Their stories hold critical elements of great influence in shaping young girls' attitudes, awareness, and direction in their schooling and career choices. The personal characteristics found in their stories are faith, determination, and intelligence.

Faith comes across in stories about how the women have resorted to a spiritual belief in order to bear their struggles with immigration issues, learning a new culture, and underemployment in a new society.

Determination is a quality that runs through many of the personal narratives told to the daughters. The mothers have pushed past what they perceived to be limitations and barriers to forge ahead with strength against odds to provide their daughters, and their families as a whole, the best possible opportunities for a better life than they experienced in Mexico.

Intelligence is too often confused with attainment of formal schooling, but in reality, intelligence is what we do with the knowledge we have. The stories that these women tell their daughters show their true intelligence in their ability to interpret the complex society in which they live and raise their families. Mothers manage a household and support a family with fewer financial resources than they need to live comfortably. This requires a great deal of intelligence. The decisions they make on a daily basis are needed to resolve family problems.

The University's Role

Schools participating in a Mother/Daughter program forge partnerships with a local university, which sponsors five key activities during the year: (a) campus open house and tour, (b) career day, (c) summer camp at the university campus, (d) tutorial support, and (e) leadership conference.

Campus open house and tour. This is the first visit to a university campus for the mother and daughter participants. Both mothers and daughters indicate that the visit to the university is the participants' favorite part of the program.

Career day. Outstanding Latina professional women from the community come to the university campus and speak to the mother and daughter participants about the importance of education and strategies for educational success.

At career day, mothers learn to become more effective role models for their daughters. Mothers increase their awareness and use of community resources and develop positive self-esteem and confidence as they learn about the possible postsecondary options available to their daughters. The girls become acquainted with careers

> ### *Elementary and Secondary*
> # SUGGESTION
> ## Career Day Activities
> - Develop Latino students' knowledge of career choices
> - Provide students and parents information about the educational track to follow for their desired career

involving higher education, especially nontraditional careers in math and science fields. They also become acquainted with professional and community role models. The girls increase their aspirations for higher education and career opportunities.

Summer camp. At the university campus, the girls participate in an intensive, two-day immersion in a full range of university activities, with the hope of giving the girls a well-rounded view and appreciation of campus life.

Tutorial support. To assure that project participants achieve required academic standards, tutorial support and leadership development are provided. College students and teachers provide tutorial support to girls in math, reading, and English language development. The volunteer college students come from the local community and state colleges. These university students are role models and mentors who facilitate learning and retention in school.

Leadership conference. Another important component of the MD program is the development of leadership skills that come from first-hand involvement in leadership activities. These are skills the girls need as they become productive members of the community with a responsibility to improve the community's quality of life.

Students work with sponsoring teachers, district coordinators, and program staff members to identify, plan, carry out, and document selected community projects, which they present at the scheduled annual leadership conference. The project's leadership conference provides participants the opportunity to develop their leadership skills in planning, budgeting, organizing, negotiating, and risk taking; in the process, they gain confidence and increase self-esteem.

The girls develop a wide variety of service projects for their community. For example, to improve school attendance, one or more students might organize a school attendance campaign involving students, parents, faculty, staff, and community members.

Building Confidence

How young Latinas perceive their personal power has much to do with their relationship with their mothers. Surveys with the Mother/Daughter program girls have thus far indicated that they listen to and depend on their mothers for guidance about school and career decisions. Although the girls know that their mothers did not have formal education in the United States—or in Mexico, in some cases—they go to their mothers for advice first before turning to their friends or teachers. Mothers are the ones to direct the girls to find the appropriate resources. Often, through the personal stories they share with their daughters, they make the girls look within for the confidence to resolve problems in a new way.

When the girls are asked if they choose their mothers as their confidantes, they say yes. Specifically, they appreciate the stories they have heard about how their mothers managed during hard times. This makes the girls believe that their mothers are knowledgeable, even if the mother did not have a great deal of formal schooling.

Secondary

PERSONAL VIGNETTE

I recall one time when things weren't going well for me in my first year of high school. It was all just too stressful, and I felt nervous about my grades. My mother had stopped helping me with my homework years before because she didn't know how to do the homework that I had to do. She hadn't finished school in Mexico, and her English wasn't the best. Anyway, she noticed that I was feeling pretty down about things. Then I told her about the stress

I had and how I didn't know if I could handle high school especially because I want to go to college, which will be more difficult.

Mom was very understanding. She sat me down at the kitchen table, and she shared about going to school in Mexico at a time when her family was very poor, and she wasn't sure that she'd be able to stay in school and work to help her family. Mom told me that she was so excited about learning, but her mom needed her to help work the farm when her father died. Gosh, Mom was just 10 years old, and all of her brothers and sisters were younger. Anyway, Mom told me about how her mother didn't want her to leave school, but she couldn't do everything by herself. So together her mother and my mom decided that they would divide the work in the farm so that Mom did most of her share before school, after school, and on weekends. Her mother would let her stay in school as long as the work got done. My mom felt so glad that she could stay in school that she studied hard and managed to work and go to school.

Mom's story made me feel that I could do what I needed to do to make it in school as long as I loved learning and could get Mom to help me work through things just like her mom helped her. At least, I don't have to work hard in the fields. Actually, that's what Mom told me. She said, "You don't ever have to feel that you're doing this alone. None of us are alone. Even if I don't know how to help you to do the work that you're required to do, I will help you find the tutors at school, or I'll talk with your counselor to show me what I need to do. So don't ever feel that you can't talk to me." That made me feel so much better. I wasn't as afraid. I felt more confident.

From the mothers' stories, girls learn to trust their own strength and have confidence in themselves and to think about what they must do to go to college and have a better education.

The teacher/mother support component of the Mother/Daughter program involves all of the teachers working with parents in establishing and sustaining an academically supportive environment in the girls' home. When the parents enter the program, they and the teachers sign a contract to participate actively for the duration of the program. The teachers communicate regularly with parents through phone calls.

The teachers and school staff guide mothers in working with their daughters to raise academic achievement and serve as role models.

Elementary and Secondary

SUGGESTION

Effective Communication Between Teachers, Specialists, and Parents Involves Conducting Workshops on ...

- Homework
- Good study skills
- Discipline at home and school
- Discussions about colleges and universities
- How to fill out applications for elementary and secondary scholarships to private high schools and academies and scholarships to academic summer school programs and colleges

In the teacher/mother meetings, the following topics are explored: (a) the nature of the expectations developed for the pursuit of postsecondary academic goals and careers, (b) what the parent needs to do to facilitate the academic development of her daughter, and (c) what kinds of school and community resources can be accessed by parents to support their daughters' academic performance in school.

For the mothers, one of the highlights of the Mother/Daughter program is that they have experienced a strong sense of growth. Developing mothers' aspirations for their own personal and professional growth is an important part of the teacher/parent component. The mothers involved in the Mother/Daughter program learn to become leaders. They gain confidence to stand in front of a group and address other women and to teach them ways to advocate in school for their children. In many cases, the mothers of the girls in the program report feeling so inspired by their daughters' enthusiasm for learning that they return to school themselves to complete high school. Some move on to community college to improve their English before transferring to a state university for the bachelor's degree, as is the case of Alma Garcia.

Elementary and Secondary

PERSONAL VIGNETTE

Alma Garcia's daughter began the Mother/Daughter program in the fifth grade.

Participating with the Mother/Daughter program has taught me what it means to be supportive of my daughter, Marina. Although I felt that I had been supportive before, for Marina, it was fine with her to do the very least to get by. But this group taught me how to get my daughter motivated and to go the extra mile. Just doing "good" work isn't enough to get into college and pursue a career. I've had to learn how to get my daughter inspired to do the best that she can. That's why talking constantly with her teachers has been the best support net that my daughter has had. She knows that we're all in this together with her. That extra push for Marina has been the constant contact with the other girls who can commiserate with her about not liking school but still having to do the best work possible.

By the time that my daughter was in her first year of high school, she was so turned on about school that she began pushing me to get my diploma and enroll in college. So I've done that. I am now enrolled at the state college and working toward my psychology major. What's great is that our getting involved in the Mother/Daughter program helped my daughter, and then she inspired me to go to college. We both laugh at the thought of graduating from college together. It may just happen.

[Translated from Spanish]

Funding

Multiple funding sources are needed to implement a program like the Mother/Daughter program. The programs in Tempe, Arizona; San Mateo, California; Albuquerque, New Mexico; and El Paso, Texas, use federal grants, local foundation funds, and local school district appropriations to ensure that all of the components come together. Although funding is critical in getting the program initiated, schools, school districts, and communities first need to make a commitment to put in place a comprehensive program to benefit Latino students in getting to college.

SUMMARY

- Attending college and university requires early knowledge, goal setting, and informed planning, and Latino students and parents need to learn that it is possible for them to attain this.

- Elementary, middle, and secondary schools need to socialize and orient male and female Latino students to focus on their academic achievement to enter college.
- Mentors can tutor and assist students through middle and secondary school to learn good study skills and remain attentive to their academic achievement.
- Latino parents without college background need parent education on what they need to do to guide their children through middle and high school, with college as the bigger purpose.

7

Designing Schoolwide Parent Involvement Programs

M odels of parent involvement uniquely depend on resources particular to a community. No single model can ensure a successful partnership between Latino families and educators. As they take steps to establish a systematic program to enlist parent involvement, schools need to restructure all of their methods to create maximum contact between schools and families. Building a system to support parent involvement in a school must embrace the whole organization, supporting and linking the strengths and isolated endeavors of individuals. One size does not fit all where parent involvement programs are concerned. Successful programs harness the local talent in their respective communities (Lucas et al., 1990).

Schools that have effective parent-involvement relationships with the Latino community operate with strong systematic programs. Components vary from school to school depending on the size of the district, the historic and political presence of Latinos in the community, and the extent to which schools commit resources.

While successful parent-involvement programs need to be tailored to their community, good ones share certain characteristics that are consistent with the fundamentals of parent involvement discussed earlier. First, successful programs begin by assessing the school's training needs for classroom teachers, other staff, and Latino parents. School needs are assessed and determined by a collective of people from these three arenas. The collective effort begins from this starting point. Second, parent involvement programs need to be sensitive to language issues. In some schools, elaborate efforts have been made to involve parents, but they exclude Spanish-speaking and other language groups.

The issue of schools with multicultural populations needs to be addressed before moving on to the strategies for organizing a parent involvement program. Although it is impractical and unnecessary for schools to design a separate parent-involvement program for each cultural group, a school can provide specific things for each group to ensure their maximum participation. Written and verbal communication with parents in their respective home language is essential. The specific cultural community needs to be contacted to maximize support for teachers and other school educators so they can understand the particular cultural group. Within these parameters—using the language and contacting local community leaders—schools can design parent involvement programs that unite all parents to work together on behalf of their children and in support of the school, as discussed in the remainder of this chapter.

CONNECTING

Commitment and Attitudes

To connect with Latino families in a strong partnership, educators need to have a foundation that is committed to working with Latino parents to bring about the highest level of academic achievement for Latino students. The attitudes that most enable this to occur begin with recognizing that there is an equal partnership between parents and educators. That is, attitudes that most promote successful collective efforts in a parent involvement plan are those that allow for diverse thinking and different ways of participating in the schools. Affirmative attitudes about parents' role in education lead to parent involvement. Most important is the attitude that places negotiation center stage. Educators need to involve parents on all issues that affect children. The idea is to prevent problems as much as possible.

SHARING INFORMATION

Purpose and Policy

At the center of a strong parent-involvement program is a mission statement explicitly stating that the school district values sharing power between educators and Latino families. Visions of how a district and every school within it want students to succeed academically are reflected in this part of their parent involvement policy. For example, if a school district asserts high expectations that all Latino students will graduate from high school, this should be specified in the plan. One key goal is to expect that all students and families will receive information to help them prepare to attend college, beginning in the intermediate grades.

Goal setting involves short-term and incremental plans that allow programs a reasonable time to accomplish the activities that move toward the school district's main purpose.

Elementary and Secondary

POINT

Basic Needs in Planning a Schoolwide Program

- Educators should involve Latino parents
- Attitudes affirming diversity, collectivity, and possibility set the tone for strong school–family–community relationships
- Visible messages welcoming parents across the school district create a supportive environment

---

Elementary and Secondary

POINT

Together, Parents and Educators Can ...

- Share power
- Expand their knowledge, develop new skills, and make change
- Hold visions for productive partnerships leading to high educational opportunities for all students

---

Personnel

When hiring personnel to work with Latino parents, schools need to take into account bilingual expertise. Personnel can be trained by the school district so that resources are shared at a district level, at local

Elementary and Secondary

POINT

To Create Strong Partnerships Between Educators and Parents...

- Promote training to solve differences
- Remain open to possibilities of changing the way things have been done traditionally
- Network with other Latino parent groups to build coalitions and accomplish common goals

community colleges, and at night school. In some cases, local college instructors may be contracted to teach educators in their school setting about (a) attitudes, (b) language and communication, and (c) strategies in parent education including parenting skills, homework, and family literacy. The areas that need to be strengthened in parent education include attitudes and communication with schools.

Superintendents play a central role in planning and executing districtwide parent-involvement plans in each school. Their leadership sets the climate and expectations for all other district principals, teachers, and support staff to commit to a systematic parent-involvement program in the school.

After receiving a doctoral degree in education from the University of Southern California, Dr. Daniel Seda (a pseudonym), an African American, became the assistant superintendent for secondary instruction in the Santa Barbara High School District. Upon his arrival in the school district, he formed a council of parents representing various interests in the community. He met with the parent groups monthly. In those meetings, he solicited their views on current issues while he shared his own vision of education for the district's students. During that time, he continued speaking at community agencies and conducting workshops to train parents to work more effectively with schools and to learn ways to help their children reach greater academic success.

After his position as an assistant superintendent, Dr. Seda became Superintendent in Carpinteria. He remained connected with the Carpinteria community at large through his column in local newspapers, where he communicated his perspectives on education. Here Dr. Seda speaks about the importance of working closely with parents and the community.

Secondary and Elementary

CASE EXAMPLE

As a superintendent, I proposed and funded a series of workshops for the Spanish-speaking Latino families. The plan was for Dr. Santana, a Spanish-speaking child development consultant, to educate Latino parent leaders, who would in turn instruct other parents on topics of child development. Dr. Santana instructed Latino parent leaders on child development and finding strengths of the family. The leaders who received training with Dr. Santana in turn organized other parents and extended the pool of informed Latino parent leaders. The second tier of trainees then selected a third group to train.

Principals also became more engaged with their respective school-site Latino parent groups. I made it my objective to hold all administrators accountable for creating strong parent-involvement programs with Latino and non-Latino parents. In evaluating school principals, I held them responsible for instituting strong family and school relationships. Together, principals, teachers, and parent leaders reached out to other Latino families who felt isolated and convinced them that they, too, could get involved in the schools and become leaders.

People have unique inner power, and it's my expectation that they use all of their potential to make sure that all students succeed in school. I've seen that Latino parents also hold those expectations, and they share these expectations with each other in their Latino parent organization. Cooperation is one of the values inherent in the empowerment process. I make it a point to write a column in the local newspaper so that the community stays informed about what we're doing and how I see things in the district.

In my article, *Winning Isn't Always Defeating Somebody*, I discuss the nature of competition in our society and how it poses many hard questions about its effect on us as a society, how we think about our potential, about each other's ability, and how we relate to each other given the power of these values. I have strong feelings about the meaning of competition and cooperation. I believe that as a society, we're preconditioned to compete, and people usually interpret that to mean that someone must lose. Too little attention is

(Continued)

(Continued)

given to the concept of win/win. The notion is considered one of settling for less than we can have. Some believe that if we don't emphasize winning and losing, then we're not serious about the thing we want.

We're hooked on winning because it brings us happiness. We jump, we cheer, we laugh, and our disposition improves. However, when we lose, the opposite occurs. But what happens when we lose? There's a general impulse to dismiss it as a loss by saying, "It is just a game anyway."

Labeling ourselves as winners or losers is commonplace and defines the way that schools classify students during their entire school career. After a loss, we reassess so that we can turn our defeat into a future victory. We want to rank ourselves so we can tell others we are at the top. Of course, when one is at the top, someone must be at the bottom. It is OK to rank students when one is among the top, but how would we like to be 499th out of 500? Where does it say that we must have so many As, so many Bs, Cs, Ds, and Fs? School is not a football game where for one to win, another one must lose!

School can and should be a place where all can succeed, where all can win. There should be nothing wrong with all students earning As. If we truly believe that education is the answer to our society's problems, then we would want all classes, all schools, and all districts to win. We all win in education when all students learn and reach their potential.

What students need is a different orientation to winning. Schools need to teach children that life is not a game about winning or losing arguments, scoring points, winning games, or collecting toys. Winning in life is about living full out, going for our potential, reaching for the stars, being a good person, giving all we have to give, and loving everyone with all our heart and soul. That's really winning!

NOTE: This Case Example and others in this chapter are based on interviews, observations, and case files assembled by the author over the course of a 25-year career. In some cases, names have been changed to protect privacy, but any quotations are substantially the words of the original speaker, and the incidents occurred as described.

Leadership, under Dr. Seda's administration, emphasized a commitment to motivate others to make the same promise to education that he brought to Carpinteria. His philosophy of education began with appraising his own strengths and incorporating his preference to negotiate in a collective way. Collectively, cooperation, excellence, and forthright communication and inclusion were values congruent with those of the Latino parent organization and leadership.

Connections among children, parents, and teachers, which Dr. Seda promoted, were dynamic and real in people's lives. These sectors of the community exist interdependently with each other, and each has a responsibility to work with the others for the common purpose of providing Latino students the optimal opportunity to learn, stay in school, graduate from high school, and attend college.

STAYING INVOLVED

Designing a Program

The balancing act relative to parent involvement is always about representing the ideal while making it work in the real world. There are imperative components of all parent involvement programs that can be combined to function as a coordinated system toward common ends. Figure 7.1, Components of a School-Level Parent Education Program, arranges the areas of parent involvement that intersect in a comprehensive plan, bridging all the groups of educators and parents who need to collaborate through well-articulated planning, policies, and training.

For an effective parent-involvement plan, everyone in the school district, from the superintendent to the teacher assistant, needs to be involved in a district's parent involvement program. Whether it is daily face-to-face interaction or working with policy, everyone in the district office deals with issues that at some point impact students and their families. Therefore, in designing a district parent-involvement program, all school-level educators need to be committed to the process.

How an urban district with this enrollment and ethnic composition organizes its parent involvement program is illustrated in the example below. The Stockton Unified School District's model, the Parent Resource Center, provides parent involvement services for all its K through 12 schools. Stockton is a city about 50 miles south of Sacramento. The school district enrollment in kindergarten through 12th grade is about 32,000. The school district's ethnic composition is

Figure 7.1   Components of a School-Level Parent Education
Program

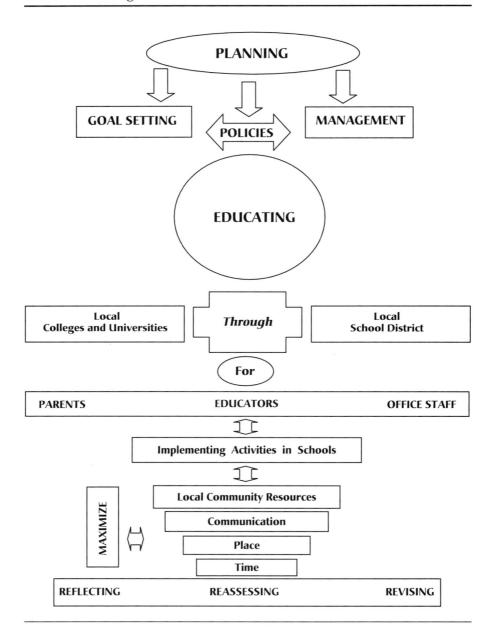

40% Latino, 29% Asian American, 17% White, 13% African American,
and 2% Native American. The Parent Resource Center has succeeded
in its goals to involve parents. Its features are delineated in the
following case example (Paige & Betka, 2001).

Elementary and Secondary

CASE EXAMPLE

How the Stockton Parent Resource Center
Involves Parents

- Transportation and child care are provided to parents attending meetings and events at the center.
- Parents have access to resource materials (videos, books, etc.) they can use at the center or at home, that is, curriculum materials to use with children.
- Information is available about state and federally funded programs in the district.
- Parenting classes and workshops in math and literacy are offered.

Evidence of Success

- Mentoring parents train both parents and school staff.
- Parent volunteers have increased in the schools.
- Funding for the center comes from Title I federal and state funds.
- Several parents trained in the center have become school board members and advocates of parent involvement in national educational organizations.
- Outstanding parent volunteers are honored each year for their service to the schools.

In the Stockton Parent Resource Center, Latino parents who speak more English than Spanish get more involved in policy-making groups, whereas Latino parents who speak more Spanish than English attend more workshops and parenting classes. Directors of this center note that Latino parents are more inclined to attend local school-site meetings and events held at night than they are to attend evening classes or events at the Parent Resource Center. Having to drive a longer distance and leave families for a slightly longer period of time is cited as a possible explanation. An ongoing parent committee assists in evaluating the management of the center and considers how to plan events to maximize attendance of all ethnic groups.

In an effective parent-involvement program, parents are equal partners in planning, participation, and management of the school district's parent involvement program. In some cases, Latino parents are not very active when the district announces its interest in planning a program. If Latino parents are not as active prior to the development of a district parent-involvement program, educators can reach out to active parents and local Latino organizations with knowledge of the Latino community and family needs.

Planning parent involvement for school districts and individual school sites is a continuous process. It is ongoing and fluid, subject to modifications as the needs change in the schools and in the communities. Crucial to the planning process are the central goals supported by the district at large, as well as all the individual schools. Short-term and incremental goals have a place in the big picture of the district parent-involvement program. The ongoing process of educator-parent communication builds support for children's highest academic achievement. Focus group meetings are held to reflect about and agree on goals and activities and to learn about the community and assess needs, strengths, and skills. Through this process, leaders are identified who can take charge of specific components of the parent involvement program.

The Wendell Phillips Magnet School in Kansas City, Missouri, is an urban school designed with desegregation funds. Its student population is about 70% African American, 22% white, and 8% Latino or other minority. Wendell Phillips School serves about 400 students in kindergarten through fifth grade. In this model of parent involvement, it is important to note how this school district with multiple ethnic communities keeps parents involved when Latinos are not the majority group (Paige & Betka, 2001). Funding for this magnet school's parent involvement program comes from Title I, state desegregation funds, community volunteers, and contributions from local businesses.

Elementary

CASE EXAMPLE

How the Wendell Phillips Magnet School Involves Parents

- A parent resource area lends parents kits, videos, books, and other educational materials.

- Home visits are conducted to discuss children's academic or social performance.
- Carpools or transportation by taxi is arranged to get parents to school.

Evidence of Success

- Attendance at informational meetings is more than 150 parents.
- The first, third, and fourth grade have made slight gains in percentile points on standardized tests.
- More parents attend parent-teacher conferences each year.

Training is essential in ensuring the effectiveness of any program. Just as teachers require continuous training to keep current on effective teaching, so do parents and educators need instruction on how to communicate with each other. Latino parents, in particular, need education about the U.S. schooling system since many did not themselves go to American schools. In training school staff to work with Latino parents, more than language needs to be considered. How school staff interacts with parents has much to do with the attitudes held about Latinos. Staff members sometimes believe that parents have more information than they actually have about the way that schools operate. Office staff workers are an invaluable part of a school because they hold a wealth of information about students and school personnel that parents should know. However, this resource is not always available to all parents. Often, parents have difficulty with the school because they do not have all the information they need about the various professionals and how they all play a role in their children's schooling. At times, parents just want to know how to get another child to stop hitting their child. They expect the office staff to have all the answers, so it is important for staff workers to convey that all students are valued and that the problem being resolved merits their attention.

To maintain positive relations between the school and Latino parents, school staffs need to dispense information in a language parents understand and direct the parents to the appropriate professional responsible for their child's welfare. In communicating with Latino parents, office staffs should speak the parents' language or have someone available to them to translate. Getting the correct information to the parents in their own language makes all the difference in the world.

In Texas, Hueco Elementary School in the Socorro Independent School District is an exemplary rural school where parents are actively involved. The school has an enrollment of about 600 students, 98% of them Latino (Paige & Betka, 2001).

Elementary

CASE EXAMPLE

How Hueco School Involves Parents

- Communication with the home is done in Spanish and English (bilingually).
- Teachers are allowed release time to conduct home visits.
- Workshops and courses are provided on parenting skills, effective parenting, child development, drug abuse, and health.
- Parents have incentives to read with their children.
- A Parent Communication Council of 30 parents meets with the principal monthly.
- All workshops and meetings are conducted bilingually.

Evidence of Success

- Test scores are above the 70th percentile in all areas of the Texas Assessment of Academic Skills.
- Student attendance averages 97%.
- Parents participate in school decision making and classroom instruction, advancing their own educational goals, which contributes to student learning at home.

In this model of parent involvement, schools like Hueco with a high Latino student enrollment can organize effective parent involvement consistent with the principles of successful parent participation.

Implementing parent involvement activities for Latino parents in the schools requires a systematic approach that coordinates time, place, and communication to facilitate Latino parents' attendance. What is convenient for school personnel is not always feasible for Latino parents. Many of them work long hours at two or three jobs. If their attendance is important for the schools, then the schools must learn the most convenient time for parents in that community to attend meetings. Although some schools find it impossible to get parents to attend Friday evening meetings, other schools find that Latino parents actually prefer Friday evening meetings because they do not need to help their children with homework on that night. While many parents work on Saturdays, they may not have to be up as early.

Location of any school event, especially those held in the evening, needs to be accessible to Latino parents. Often, schools hold meetings in church halls, community centers, or public libraries to accommodate parents who would otherwise need to take several buses or other forms of public transportation to the nearest school.

The Rodney B. Cox Elementary School in Dade City, Florida, offers an example of how this pre-kindergarten through fifth grade urban school with 44% Latino enrollment organizes its parent involvement program. Other ethnic groups in the school include 40% African American and 16% white (Paige & Betka, 2001).

Elementary

CASE EXAMPLE

How the Cox Schoolwide Program Involves Parents

- The school's open door policy ensures that teachers can meet with parents whenever they visit the school.
- A parent involvement coordinator, migrant home-school coordinators, and a minority recruiter make home visits and train parents.
- Monthly parent workshops are conducted by school staff to discuss parenting skills and assisting with homework.
- Counseling and health and dental care are provided to students and their families.

Evidence of Success

- A steady flow of volunteers works daily in the school and classrooms.
- More than 100 parents participate in workshops monthly.
- Test scores have increased since 1995, and more students are scoring above the 50th percentile.

The Cox school model of parent involvement places a value on communication with parents, whether at school or in the home. Educators engage parents in various types of activities. Mobilizing parents is only the first step; engaging them in the conversation, whether it is a meeting or a festival, requires the events to be held in the language they comprehend. Once parents are present at an event, communicating with them is the basis of all parent-involvement efforts.

Reflecting, reassessing, and revising parent involvement programs are not processes that should happen only once a year. The effectiveness of a program rests on the continuous reassessment and revision of the various components of the program. Making a district-level parent-involvement strategy work means having an action plan in place, but making it flexible enough to accommodate the target audience. There is nothing worse than planning a great show and not having anyone attend because they could not make it at that time or place and would not understand a word if they did attend. In all three of these arenas—time, place, and language of communication—the school needs to know its community's needs and make the meetings and events accessible.

SUMMARY

- How schools and school districts determine the success and outcomes of their parent involvement program depends on the activities designed by the school district.
- Most frequently, educators are concerned with how many Latino parents attend meetings, workshops, and conferences, but the effectiveness of these activities cannot always be judged by sign-in attendance alone.
- Educators and parents need to identify techniques to measure participation and interactions with each other.
- Many parent-involvement strategies impact parent interactions with their children and educators in important ways, generating more meaningful information about processes to involve, inform, and train parents.
- A systematic evaluation captures these successes, either by asking parents to respond in writing or through focus group discussions.
- In organizing Latino parents, educators need to identify ways they can interact with Latino parents most effectively.

- It is imperative for districts to understand what will change as a result of the parent involvement program.
- In addition to documenting the quality and effectiveness of a parent involvement program, school districts need to remember that all change takes time. When one problem is solved, another one will emerge because parent involvement is a process without a beginning and end.
- Therefore, organization of the school and the school district's programs needs to be under continuous review and revision. Successful partnerships require flexibility to maintain an open conversation between parents and educators.

8

Forming School-Family-Community Partnerships

E ducators play a central role in community organizations that work toward educational reform at the local or state level. Community-driven school reform, with its focus on parent organizing, has as its purpose improving student opportunities to succeed academically. Latino and other ethnic-group parents have organized and influenced educational improvements from the top down and from the bottom up. That is, there are parent/community organizations that are community-based, and while they serve the local community, they have expanded statewide and nationally. As such, they influence educational policy at all levels, from the local community to the state legislature. From building leadership among parents to building collaborative relationships between parents and school leaders, organizations attempt to effect change in the schools from the top down through policies. Latino parents also effect change in the schools through organizing the grassroots community, one parent at a time. Countless well-organized community, state, and national programs exist to support Latino and diverse ethnic mobilization to improve their living conditions. I have chosen only three here to illustrate the impact of top-down and bottom-up change in schools.

The central focus of community-driven school reform is that community organizing creates the social capital necessary to form equal partnerships between the community and the schools. Community organizations enable less represented groups to break through the school system's bureaucracy. Helping to create public policy while obtaining resources and eliminating disparity among groups in the school and in the community are goals of community-driven school reform.

> *Elementary and Secondary*
>
> # POINT
>
> ## Some Ways Community-Driven Latino Groups Assist Schools
>
> - Improving communication with teachers
> - Helping high school students stay in school
> - Keeping students' identity strong
> - Supporting high school students to graduate and pursue college

The three programs featured in this chapter, PICO, COPLA, and College Track, represent three important types of community-driven organizations. These groups count on partnerships with schools to expand the academic success of poor and ethnically diverse students in elementary and secondary schools.

NATIONAL NETWORKING FOR ASSISTING LOCAL SCHOOLS

In the late 1990s, the California State Legislature passed a law that capped the primary classroom enrollment at 20 students. That effort was largely spearheaded by the interfaith parent organization, PICO.

PICO is the acronym for Pacific Institute for Community Organization. It is a national umbrella organization for 45 local interfaith groups that link up across 12 states. All local organizations begin at local churches and belong to the larger umbrella organization, PICO. An example of a local organization is the Oakland Community Organization (OCO). Active parents organize themselves to address issues pertaining to the health, safety, education, and overall well-being of the families in the neighborhood. PICO's role is to assist local communities in creating parent organizations with the power to improve the quality of family life and neighborhoods. Depending on the issue being addressed, whether it is housing safety, school violence, or the student dropout rate, OCO parents meet with the mayor, chief of police, or school superintendent. The meetings are well publicized and well attended. A major reason for the large attendance is that parents of all language groups can understand the issues because translation is provided in people's respective languages. The goal is to inform the community about the issue and to have the public officials there to answer questions and to strategize a plan for the particular need.

For new community projects, PICO initially assists local organizations to raise funds and to recruit and train community organizers. PICO also helps local organizations in their evaluation and ongoing assessment through on-site visits, formal assessments, and regular written and verbal communications.

PICO provides leadership training seminars and technical assistance for parents of diverse cultural and religious backgrounds who share common values for creating a socially responsive community. Principles that drive the PICO organizing efforts are (a) respect for human dignity, (b) creation of a just society, and (c) development of the whole person. These principles undergird the actions of the national as well as the local community groups.

For example, with respect to the educational agenda of OCO, parents of diverse backgrounds have worked together for 25 years. In interviews, community leaders, including school community liaisons, emphasize working with educators to build strong schools. Latino parents become involved in OCO through their respective churches, where the community organizing efforts begin for all parents in the OCO group.

Christina's story of community activism is a fairly typical one among the Latino parents involved in OCO. Up until the time that Christina immigrated to the United States, she lived in Guadalajara, where she worked with the poor through the Catholic Church. As a young immigrant woman in Oakland, she attended her local church, St. Elizabeth, which is where she got involved with OCO. At that time, Christina was very discontented with the school district's handling of her daughter's year-round program. She attended a meeting at the parish where OCO representatives described their various projects, including safe housing, and discussed contacting the public school superintendent about creating afterschool programs for children who were getting into trouble because they were unsupervised.

Christina immediately got involved with OCO. She smiles as she tells how her first activist job was in her own household, to liberate herself from her husband (quotes are translated from Spanish). "He didn't like me going out at night, so when I began attending OCO meetings, I told him that I was attending a church meeting," she said. "That part was true since OCO met at St. Elizabeth." She soon learned the benefits of becoming active in the schools. She became acquainted with the good teachers who were willing to help her daughter excel. By the time that her daughter got to middle school, one of her teachers helped her to get a full scholarship to a private girls' school. By working within the school system through OCO, Christina is able to understand how change happens and what needs to get done to bridge the home-school divide.

"Many educators support OCO parents' efforts in the schools because they see how having smaller classes improves children's learning," she said. "But there are some personnel who resist the parents in the schools and would rather continue doing things as they have traditionally. They're comfortable with their old ways. We need to help them become more comfortable with change."

At the time that interviews with Christina were collected, the California state budget had been decimated, and schools faced severe cuts in teaching staff and programs. Christina feared that the programs put in place through OCO's efforts in Oakland schools are in peril. Her most urgent message to educators is

Educators need to let go of fear. Sometimes they see Latino and other parents as a threat. But OCO does not exist to remove teachers or administrators from their positions or jobs. The organization exists to collaborate and to make the educators' work easier. And together we can help our children get the best education possible.

How educators can assist educational efforts through community organizations is something that is clear to the OCO parents. They have seen the fruits of collaborative efforts when the school district educators listen to OCO's concerns and, together, they can strategize for a win-win solution to an education and community problem. To OCO parents, everyone in the schools has a role to play in supporting OCO school-parent partnerships, whether they are personnel in the central administration office or staff directly involved in children's daily instruction in the local schools. Educators who make policy decisions can support OCO's proposals.

In the schools, administrators, teachers, community liaisons, and office staff deal with parents and students every day. They can

Elementary and Secondary

POINT

Organizational Features of PICO

- *Size.* Involves local communities of interfaith and multiethnic adults that unite across 12 states
- *Cost.* Funded by nonprofit foundations, school district support, and programs in school reform
- *Mission.* Collaborates with school districts to improve education for poor diverse communities
- *Purpose.* Develops parent leadership and activities for students

Elementary and Secondary

SUGGESTION

Educators Can Assist Community-Driven Organizations Like OCO by ...

- Becoming informed about community-driven organizations that serve the school community and how they forge relationships with the schools
- Visibly welcoming culturally diverse parents in the schools
- Negotiating with parent groups to improve family and parent education
- Providing fiscal support to programs for community-school partnerships
- Advocating in favor of parent-initiated projects to better facilitate learning opportunities
- Accommodating afterschool programs for students in elementary and secondary schools

support parents in making the necessary changes to maximize children's learning opportunities to succeed in school socially and academically.

Some of the effective changes that have resulted from collaborations between OCO and the Oakland schools have been in the area of program development. Large schools make academic achievement difficult for many students, especially Latinos and other children who are academically at risk. In Oakland, OCO parents have successfully worked with the school district administration to create smaller elementary schools and to develop afterschool programs and, in the case of the high schools, to create smaller theme schools to allow students to focus more specifically on areas of their strengths.

Families have learned about their rights and responsibilities pertaining not only to the educational system but also to other institutions in the community, enhancing their lives by engaging proactively. OCO continues to help families in the community to appreciate their diversity and potential for being active members in their children's education, as well as in the community as a whole.

GRASSROOTS ORGANIZING FOR LATINO PARENT INVOLVEMENT

The Latino community in Carpinteria, California, faced social, cultural, economic, and educational isolation from the white Euro-American community. Although English-speaking Latinos had attained some professional positions in town, many Spanish-speaking Latinos experienced inequality and institutional discrimination. That is, Latino parents organized a grassroots organization and received strong support from a couple of school district educators.

Secondary

CASE EXAMPLE

Mrs. Avila, a parent, recalls her experience with her son, Raul. When I interviewed her, Raul had just been promoted to the fourth grade. Mrs. Avila talked about her difficulty in helping her son improve his reading skills.

> Raul was in the third grade and read only in Spanish. But when he began learning to read in English, he had many problems. He was not doing well, and his teacher, Mrs. Robins, called me. She also sent home notes with Raul and told him to tell me to call him. But I felt so embarrassed, thinking that it was my fault, that I just kept trying to help my son as much as possible at home by myself.

> Weeks passed and the teacher just continued working with Raul. At home, his mother knew that he was having problems: "I just did not understand his homework. I was unable to help him because

(Continued)

(Continued)

the instructions were confusing even though they were in Spanish." The reports sent home by the teacher never reached Mrs. Avila because Raul feared giving them to her. His mother, on the other hand, felt that she was to blame: "I felt kind of ashamed that I couldn't help Raul since my schooling was so limited. That kept me from going to the school and talking to Mrs. Robins."

The distance grew between Raul and his mother, as well as between Mrs. Avila and Mrs. Robins. The breakdown in communication isolated everyone in a way that made them work harder but minimized gains.

NOTE: This Case Example and others in this chapter are based on interviews, observations, and case files assembled by the author over the course of a 25-year career. In some cases, names have been changed to protect privacy, but any quotations are substantially the words of the original speaker, and the incidents occurred as described.

Raul's case is typical of Mexican parents' experience in the schools, not only in Carpinteria but also in other communities where I worked as a researcher. Although Raul's case is not an extremely urgent one, it is nevertheless a critical one because it becomes increasingly problematic for parents like Mrs. Avila, who remain strangers to teachers like Mrs. Robins. As their children move up in the grades, the gap between parents and schools widens. Parents feel unable to deal with the academic subject matter, and hopelessness ensues on the part of the parents when they do not know how to pursue resources to help the students. The schism between Latino families and schools is reflected in the children's underachievement and the parents' and teachers' frustrations. Both face structural limitations in dealing with each other. Teachers are limited by their poor training in working with Latino families and diverse communities. Their illiteracy and lack of understanding of the school system, on the other hand, restricts parents. Instead of understanding that the problem is one of a structural nature, parents blame themselves for their children's learning problems.

In the Carpinteria community, the Latino families look to numerous educators in the schools who are bilingual and can advocate for the students and the parents. School links to the Latino community include the director of special programs, a school principal, and a preschool teacher, all bilingual educators. They understand the needs of the parents and students because they know the reality of the dismal standardized test scores of English-speaking Latino students and the importance of parental involvement in their children's education. The educators provide Latino students and their parents with contacts and human resources to engage them in the life of the school, improving their opportunities to succeed in school. They encourage the parents to get involved.

The lack of Latino parents' participation in the schools was one of the motivating reasons in 1985 when a supportive group was organized. Seven parents began meeting to teach each other about the ways that schools operated. Together, they learned strategies to communicate with educators and to assist their children with their schoolwork at home. Within a few short months, the small group of parents had organized the Latino parents in all of the schools to join them under the title of Comité de Padres Latinos (COPLA).

Soon after the Latino parents began a dialogue about who they are and what their goals are as a group, they invited the director of special projects to meet with them. He spoke Spanish and played the broker role between the school district and the Latino community. Parents were forced to challenge their thinking about the obstacles that impede their access to resources and opportunities to learn how the schooling system works. The meetings raised parents' awareness of their strengths, which collectively began an empowerment process in the community, their families, and their personal lives. Unpredictable possibilities opened up for the group when the parents made it clear that they were willing to put aside their fears for the sake of their children. The following interaction took place during one of the first meetings held by the Latino parents who later became COPLA. Present at the initial meeting were Alicia Rosario, Roberto Marquez, Rebeca Cortina, Manuel Peña, Rosa Martinez, David Segura, Antonia Juarez, and Juan Ramirez, representing families of children in elementary and secondary schools. They thoughtfully reflected about their role as Latino parents and their responsibility for changing conditions to improve their children's educational opportunities by assisting the children in the home and becoming advocates in the schools.

Rebeca: We have many problems to confront among ourselves. That is, we cannot argue with the schools because we have neither the means nor the language with which to do it.

Antonia: I would say that the important thing is to want to do it and it is for that reason that collectively we can learn what we need to know to help our children.

Alicia: Well, we already know how to raise our children. Nobody needs to teach us how to love our children.

Roberto: It seems to me that some Latino families here do need to learn how to take care of their children because I see their young children loose on the streets and their parents are nowhere to be seen.

Alicia: That's true that some parents don't have money to pay a capable person for child care. Sometimes they [the parents] leave their children with irresponsible people.

Manuel: What I understand from what you are saying is that we have the ability to be responsible, but there are some parents who need more help.

Roberto: Many times schools have a reason to say what they do about us Mexicans because one needs to appear confident and courageous even though we don't know how to navigate the system.

Juan: Well, I wasn't going to say anything, but the truth is that since we began talking about having to go to the schools to talk to principals, I've lost a lot of sleep. I don't know how it is possible to do something like this, which I've never done before except when they call me with complaints about my oldest son.

Rebeca: You've already told us that you're afraid to go alone to the schools, and we've assured you that no one will have to go alone because we're going in a group.

Juan: I know, but even though I want the best for my children, it is difficult to do something like this in a language that I cannot speak.

Rosa: It seems to me that, even though we don't speak English and don't know the cultural ways of this country and of Carpinteria, we also have a beautiful language, and we're respectful and have a culture that is equally valuable. That is why we should present ourselves in that spirit.

Juan: Well you're right. It's true that we do have a language with which we can communicate even though it's different than English.

Alicia: I appreciate what Mrs. Martinez says because at times we feel inferior since we don't speak English well, but we're not inferior, and we need to be proud of what we can give our children. All of Mexico's history is part of us—even if we live here.

Juan: Yes, Mrs. Rosario, but why are we made to feel inferior by teachers and principals who say that our children aren't important to us because we don't attend meetings or because we arrive late to meetings and numerous other criticisms they make?

Roberto: Well, it's true because many of us act as if we're afraid of life. Why is it that we don't go to the schools if our children matter to us? We need to change those habits that impede our presence in our children's schools. Like Mrs. Marquez always told us when our children were in preschool, these are our schools so we should act responsibly.

Juan: How do we change those habits? How can we learn to speak English, which is so difficult?

Alicia: It isn't easy to change our habits. It is necessary to talk and discuss how we think. That is why we are here to help each other—it's not easy, but there is strength in unity. We should note, for example, that even though we need to learn English, we must also make the schools communicate with us in Spanish. My children have been in these schools many years, and even though they're in bilingual classes, I never see any notices sent home in Spanish.

One meeting at a time, COPLA began to bridge the gap between parents like Mrs. Avila and teachers like Mrs. Robins, in the earlier example, who had students like Raul. This organization differed in purpose from other parent groups in the school district. The Latino parents did not organize for the purpose of meeting legal mandates of the school district. Such official committees, composed primarily of white, English-speaking parents, typically organize only to deal with questions of budget and school policies. Different from these groups, COPLA parents wanted to support each other in learning how to work with the schools in an informed way and help their children in their schooling. They constructed new avenues through which the community could voice their interests and knowledge and parents could become partners with the schools.

In COPLA meetings, parents became informed about their children's educational needs. The information came through invited school personnel or from parent leaders. For Spanish-speaking students, reaching the third grade usually meant that they were transferred from bilingual classes into English-only classes. As children make the language transition, they often need much more support. Confidence, trust, and strong academic support are vital to learning a new language. However, at that point, parents withdraw from helping because they feel intimidated by the English schoolwork that their children bring home. The issue is not that the students are learning English but that parents are shut out of their learning process. The distance created between children and parents reveals the power imbalance between home and school culture. This is a boundary that the preschool teacher in the following example helped parents to cross by teaching Latino parents how to help their children to read at home.

Elementary

CASE EXAMPLE

At a COPLA meeting, Mrs. Rosales, the preschool teacher, held a short workshop on reading with children. She told parents to turn off the television and read their child a story of their choice. At the end of every page, she told them to ask their child a question about the story, for example: Where did the chickens hide from the wolf? How will they be able to escape? She emphasized, "The important thing is to keep the children engaged in the reading even if you're the one reading the story to them." Mrs. Rosales demonstrated how to hold the book and walked around asking the parents to respond to her questions.

In the same workshop, the preschool teacher modeled for the parents how to engage the children in household chores. "When you're doing chores around the house, have the children help you. Here's how you could do it when you're folding laundry." She demonstrated to the parents how to have the children sort the clothes by color and size and how to ask children questions about the task as they're doing it. For example, which is the smaller pile?

Teachers and parents work together toward the same goal of getting Spanish-speaking Latino students to learn to their maximum potential. The collaboration works in the preschool as well as in the high school.

Secondary

CASE EXAMPLE

At a high school COPLA meeting, two high school English teachers explained to the Latino parents what the school expected of the students where English is concerned and how they teach English to limited English speakers. The teachers conducted their presentation in English, and a couple of bilingual parents translated to parents who spoke only Spanish.

Before the meeting, the principal covered expenses for a nice barbecue for teachers and COPLA parents. The parents each brought a dish, and together they put together a feast before talking school business.

Roberto Marquez, a parent leader, told parents about their responsibility to know their children, support their changes in adolescence, and set limits on their time to play and work. He explained to them the need to teach children to be responsible for themselves, and then he added, "It's all part of learning."

Some of the questions that parents asked the teachers had to do with opportunities for limited English speakers to attend college when they are unable to take required courses in English. The school doesn't offer sciences or geometry or other college-prep courses in Spanish, and if the students do not learn English well enough to get into the college prep courses, then they probably will not meet the college entrance requirements.

Parents wanted to know what options limited English-speaking students have. The teachers and the principal made it clear to the parents that it was possible for Spanish-speaking students to advance into the right classes for college if they took extra English classes in high school, worked with tutors, and worked hard on their own time to learn English.

The dialogue proved productive for the parents as they became informed about the way that the school operated, as well as the

(Continued)

(Continued)

> opportunities for their children. Parents told the teachers and the principal that they wanted their students to receive better counseling about the required courses for college. The parents also emphasized the need for the school to open college-prep courses in Spanish so that Spanish speakers had equal opportunity to attend college.

COPLA parents understood the fiscal limitations that high schools face in trying to open classes in Spanish and other languages. However, they exercised their role as advocates for their children's schooling. Organizations like COPLA offer an alternative to what typically is a home-school power struggle between educators and parents. In that struggle, the school usually maintains a position of power, even though gestures are made toward giving voice to the underrepresented population. This situation called for intervention, and a partnership grew. The COPLA organization played a catalyst role in changing the power relations between home and school in the elementary, middle, and high school.

Elementary and Secondary

POINT

Organizational Features of COPLA

- *Size.* Communitywide involving all Latinos in one community; non–Latinos are welcome
- *Costs.* School district supports it by hiring the bilingual staff, holding meetings bilingually
- *Purpose.* To develop parent awareness, knowledge, and leadership
- *Goals.* Effect change to improve schooling for Latino students in elementary and secondary schools

---

COPLA's hands-on approach to change impacted the school curriculum as well as the afterschool activities. Once COPLA organized the parents in each school, they began to focus their attention on children's activities after school. The Latino parent leadership facilitated the bringing of community resources to a larger number of students, while gaining a political voice across the district. Some of the leaders began organizing afterschool groups for youth. Rebeca Cortina organized a folkloric dance group with the assistance of a dance instructor from Santa Barbara who offered classes to the children. To keep the dancers performing, Rebeca held fundraisers, including community dances on Saturday nights, to pay for the children's costumes, lessons, and transportation to activities. She also solicited Carpinteria businesses to sponsor the children's performances. Parents whose children danced in the folkloric group also often attended COPLA meetings.

The parents who helped organize the folkloric group reminded their children, "We don't want anything for ourselves, it's all for you. We can only teach you what we know." Rebeca added,

> The dance group has worked out very well. The girls who are now the dancers are the same ones who used to wander the streets. Now they don't have to hang out in the streets. There are some girls who I used to encounter on the street and I would ask them what they were doing out so late and they would tell me that they were out walking. But it wasn't a time when girls should be out walking. Now they go to the dance and from there they go home. They don't need to be on the street.

The dance group found a way to finance its activity. Girls in Rebeca's dance group paid $5 a month to dance. Local Mexican stores sponsored four to five months of dance classes for children who could not afford the classes. While some young boys held their hands behind their back and danced around young girls in the folkloric group who swirled their long skirts, other boys found soccer more to their liking. Ramon organized a soccer league for young children of three age groups, 8 to 11, 12 to 14, and 15 to 18,

Elementary and Secondary

SUGGESTION

Educators Can Assist Community-Driven Organizations Like COPLA by . . .

- Becoming informed about community-driven organizations and their goals involving education
- Presenting informational workshops to parents at their community meetings
- Contacting the community parent organization and asking about specific ways that teachers, counselors, principals, and super-intendents can support the group

but he got his brother-in-law and other people to coach because he was still quite involved in COPLA leadership and had also assumed parent directorship of the Migrant Education Program.

In 2003, COPLA celebrated 18 years of service as a strong advocacy voice for Latino students and families in Carpinteria, sustaining active parental involvement and growth in the schools.

COLLEGE TRACK COMMUNITY PROGRAM

Different from organizations that have as their mission school reform, College Track (CT), a nonprofit community-based organization, focuses on the individual student away from the school. It began operation in 1997 in East Palo Alto and expanded to Oakland, both communities in the San Francisco Bay Area. College Track supports poor and ethnically diverse high school-age young people who aspire to attend college. The program provides advocacy by advising the students on everything from studying for the SAT examinations to finding financial assistance for college.

In the two cities, about 160 students participate in the College Track program. Students begin in their first year of high school. As of this writing, the program is in its third full cycle. All of the 33 alumni from the first graduating class are attending college. All of the young people come from families whose parents work two or more jobs to keep a roof over their heads. Were it not for College Track, these students' dreams of college would remain just that. Students and the parents need to know and do a great deal to make college or university attendance a reality. From the minute students enter high school, they have to get into the courses required by colleges, practice good study habits, and receive good grades. For students who come from families where college is not a tradition, their wishes, desires, and hopes won't make college a reality without specific strategies by specialists who can mentor them. That's precisely what College Track does. It supplements whatever the high schools may provide in the way of guidance for students who are planning to attend college. Unfortunately, many high schools do not meet the students' needs because they rarely reach out to students who don't meet the profile of the college-bound student.

Some high school teachers and counselors recognize that poor and ethnically diverse students have potential but need extra support to make it through high school and college. Knowing the limitations of the high school's counseling staff, these educators refer students in the East Palo Alto area to College Track. Other students find their way to College Track through word of mouth from friends.

Secondary

PERSONAL VIGNETTE

Before Juan Jimenez began College Track, he was involved with drugs, had a child with a young woman, and had custody of the child in his family's home.

I really needed help when I got to CT. My grades were poor and I had just begun having to take care of my son. I decided that my life had to change if I was going to be responsible for my son. Then I told my counselor at the high school that I needed to get my act together. I said that I wanted to plan for my future, and in order to get a good job, I would probably have to go to college.

She told me that I didn't stand a chance of even getting through high school because I was so far behind, unless I was really serious about working hard from now on. I wanted to make it, and I knew that if I tried hard and disciplined myself, I could accomplish anything. I just needed a lot of help. So my mother, who never had any schooling, had learned from someone about the College Track program that helped kids like me.

So I was very lucky that College Track accepted me and was willing to work with me. They helped me to stay motivated in high school even when classes seemed so boring. They took us to visit colleges, and my tutor stayed in touch with me even when I didn't want to talk with him. They even helped my mother because she had to attend parent meetings on how to assist me in filling out financial forms for scholarships and things like that. Now she understands how important education is from the early years, and she can help my son.

Being in College Track was like having a safety net in case I fell from some tall building. But once I was in College Track I didn't fall. I just kept moving forward. One of the biggest things that College Track helped me with was

(Continued)

(Continued)

> scholarships. I worked for money while I was in high school, and they taught me how to apply for scholarships.
>
> I was the first ever in my family to graduate from high school. Now I'm at San Francisco State University and have a good career plan in place for when I graduate. And College Track continues helping me with tutoring and applying for more scholarships. Even though I work while in college, I still need to pay for the college expenses, and those books get pretty expensive.
>
> ---
>
> NOTE: This Personal Vignette and others in this chapter are based on interviews, observations, and case files assembled by the author over the course of a 25-year career. In some cases, names have been changed to protect privacy, but any quotations are substantially the words of the original speaker, and the incidents occurred as described.

Juan's story differs somewhat from others in College Track only in the particulars of their experience prior to beginning the program. From the minute they walk through the door at College Track, students receive orientation on what college is about and what they will have to do to prepare academically, emotionally, and socially for it. Students are assessed, and the specialists determine and design the student's plan in tutoring and counseling. Students make a contract to check in daily with College Track, to maintain a high GPA in high school, and to attend all of the meetings, tutoring, and events held by College Track. Parents, too, have a role in the program. They attend meetings where they learn how students are progressing and receive workshop training on deadlines for college and scholarship forms that need to be completed.

Secondary

PERSONAL VIGNETTE

Louisa Aguililla was in middle school when her algebra teacher told her about the College Track program. Immediately, she informed her parents about it and got herself accepted into the program even before high school began.

I had always been a good student, and since I was in elementary school, I had talked to my parents about attending college. Even then, I knew that I wanted to become a doctor, and to be one, I would have to go to college for a long time. My parents were supportive about my plans, but they worried about how they would help me to pay for my education. So when I found out about College Track, it sounded like the perfect place for me to learn how to get to college. I knew I could work hard and get pretty good grades because I want to learn, but I was a little scared about high school advanced placement classes.

College Track showed me how to get involved in community service projects because they said that it would be an important part of my application for college. Before that, I thought I needed only good grades. But with all of the activities that I got to get involved in, I also learned about myself. I got to see that I was accepting of many people who were not like me. Some lived in my same neighborhood. I learned how much confidence I had in myself to get through tough work, which made me see how I didn't get scared when things got difficult for me. I learned that it is possible to get to college and medical school.

Through afterschool and weekend tutoring, students receive one-on-one instruction on their specific academic program. Weekend field trips to local colleges and universities, along with informational group meetings on test-taking skills and filling out college applications, help students to work collectively with specialists and peers. Seven full-time academic specialists staff College Track, along with paid tutors from Stanford University and numerous volunteers.

Secondary

POINT

Organizational Features of College Track

- *Size.* 160 ethnically diverse students in two urban and suburban communities
- *Costs.* Funded by philanthropists, corporations, and foundations
- *Purpose.* To provide intense, comprehensive, individual academic assistance and information to high school students to achieve through high school and college
- *Goal.* To expand the program to several other neighboring communities

College Track offers services beyond the "drill and kill" approach, which has students bury their heads in books to excel. It prepares students to be well-rounded people intellectually, emotionally, and experientially, as Juan and Louisa have attested. Discipline for studying is not considered the only important factor in succeeding academically; other factors are working collectively with peers, engaging in community projects, traveling abroad, and learning about other parts of the world. By College Track standards, a self-motivated learner is a responsible young adult with an awareness of his or her capabilities, someone who can establish mature human relationships with others.

Although College Track is a small program, its outcome is a success story. It is intensely individualized, and for that reason, expanding resources is critical before expanding the program to include more students. Nevertheless, College Track is expecting to expand to other Bay Area cities.

On a daily basis, College Track's mission is straightforward: to get ethnically diverse students through high school, well prepared for college. This requires daily contact with the students in a rigorous and caring way. College Track provides all students with opportunities and tools to attain their hopes.

> *Elementary and Secondary*
>
> ## SUGGESTION
>
> ### Educators Can Assist Organizations Like College Track by . . .
>
> - Informing Latino high school students about local organizations that provide academic, emotional, and financial support toward college
> - Holding informational workshops for Latino parents on how to find organizational resources to assist their young people in their college pursuits

SUMMARY

- Where parent involvement is concerned, there is no one size that fits all.
- While no single model for parent involvement exists, there are some fundamental premises that effective programs have in common.

- If schools are perceived to hold the power and the community is perceived as powerless, then the schools and communities will remain oppositional to one another.
- The primary difference between community organizing and other forms of parental mobilization is that organizing requires a structure of democratic decision making on issues and vision for all children. That is very much the practice in the community- driven programs, OCO, COPLA, and College Track, which are featured here.
- By building relationships among institutions, schools, and community organizations directed toward a common goal, the school and the community organization together build power.
- Communication and flexibility undergird parent involvement. Sharing information focuses on training educators and parents and obtaining informational resources. Staying involved means assessing effects of partnerships using multiple indicators. Finally, educators as well as parents need to remember that change takes time.
- Parent involvement programs should increase academic performance. Research findings have concluded that students whose parents are not involved in their schooling are twice as likely to be at the bottom of their class and are more inclined to repeat a grade.
- When parents are involved, students are more inclined to participate in athletics and the arts, support academic learning, have good social adjustment, and strong self-esteem. Also, they are absent less often (Fuller & Olsen, 1998; Hispanic Policy Development Project, 1990).
- Effective parent-involvement programs empowering Latino families promote high aspirations for students and strong commitment to life-long learning, as well as discipline in their schoolwork.
- Above all, graduating from high school and college, then pursuing a professional career, are most likely to be life goals for students whose parents are involved in school.

For all of these reasons, schools need to remember that commitment, respect, time, and persistence on the part of educators result in lasting partnerships between Latino parents and the schools, partnerships that ultimately contribute to student academic success.

Educational and Cultural Informational and Support Resources

Every local community has its own local Latino organizations and agencies designed to assist Latino and non-Latino residents. It is advisable for educators to scout their local communities to locate the best sources of educational and cultural information. This list of resources includes regional and national offices that are widely recognized in the Latino communities. Some of them also offer education and support to educators for building relationships with Latino families and communities. It is by no means a complete list.

Association of Hispanic Arts
173 E. 116th St., 2nd Floor
New York, NY 10029
(202) 860–5445

Bilingual Foundation of the Arts
421 North Ave. #19
Los Angeles, CA 90031
(213) 225–4044

Florida Museum of Hispanic and Latin American Art
40006 Aurora St.
Coral Gables, FL 33146

La Casa de la Raza
Santa Barbara, CA 93103
(805) 965–8581

Latino Resources at the Smithsonian
Smithsonian Institution
SI Building, Room 153, MRC 010
Washington, DC 20560
www.si.edu/resource/tours/latino/start.htm

League of United Latin American Citizens (LULAC)
701 Pennsylvania Ave N.W. #1217
Washington, DC 20004
(301) 589–2222
www.lulac.org

Mexican American Legal Defense Fund (MALDEF)
Offices in: San Francisco, Los Angeles, Houston,
    Chicago, Sacramento, San Antonio
Main Office:
1717 K St. NW #311
Washington, DC 20036
(202) 293–2849

Mexican Fine Arts Center Museum
1852 W. 19th St.
Chicago, IL 60614
(312) 738–1503

National Association of Bilingual Education (NABE)
1030 15th St. NW, Suite 470
Washington, DC 20005
(202) 789–2866

National Center for English as a Second Language Literacy
    Education (NCLE)
Washington, DC
(202) 362–0700
www.cal.org/ncle

National Center for Family and Community
Southwest Educational Development Laboratory (SEDL)
www.sedl.org

National Council of La Raza (NCLR)
Washington, DC
(202) 785–1670

National Coalition for Parent Involvement in Education
Developing Family With School Partnerships:
   Guidelines for Schools and School Districts
www.ncpie.org

National Hispanic Scholarship Fund
One Sansome St., Suite 100
San Francisco, CA 94104
(415) 445–9930

Notes from Parent Involvement Research
www.sdcoe.k12.ca.us/notes/4/parent-invol.html

Puerto Rican Legal Defense and Education Fund
99 Hudson St., 14th Floor
New York, NY 10013

San Francisco Mexican Museum
www.mexicanmuseum.org

The Education of Latino Students
Washington, DC: Office of Educational Research and Improvement
www.ed.gov/offices/OERI/index.html

The Puerto Rican Cultural Heritage House, New York, NY
www.latinoarts.org

The Puerto Rican Travelling Theater Company, New York, NY
www.prtt.org

References

Ames, C., De Stefano, L., Watkins, T., & Sheldon, S. (1995a). *Teachers' school-to-home communications and parent involvement: The role of parent perceptions and beliefs* (Report No. 28). Baltimore, MD: Johns Hopkins University, Center on Families, Communities, Schools and Children's Learning.

Ames, C., DeStefano, L., Watkins, T., & Sheldon, S. (1995b, April). *Why parents became involved in children's learning: The relationship between teachers' practices and parents' beliefs and attitudes.* Paper presented at the annual meeting of the American Educational Research Association, San Francisco.

Andrade, S. J. (1982). *Young Hispanics in the United States—Their aspirations for the future: Findings from two national surveys.* Austin, TX: Center for Applied Systems Analysis.

Asher, C. (1984). *Helping Hispanic students to complete high school and enter college.* New York: Columbia University, Teachers College.

Aspiazu, G. G., Bauer, S. C., & Spillett, M. D. (1998). Improving the academic performance of Hispanic youth: A community education model. *Bilingual Research Journal, 22*(2), 1–20.

Becher, R. M. (1984). *Parent involvement: A review of research principles of successful practice.* Washington, DC: National Institute of Education.

Bermúdez, A. B., & Padrón, Y. N. (1988, Winter). University-school collaboration that increases minority parent involvement. *Educational Horizons, 66*(2), 83–86.

Bermúdez, A. B., & Padrón, Y. N. (1990, Spring). Improving language skills for Hispanic students through home-school partnerships. *Journal of Educational Issues of Language Minority Students, 6,* 33–43.

Conderman, G., & Flett, A. (2001, September). Enhance the involvement of parents from culturally and linguistically diverse backgrounds. *Intervention in School and Clinic, 37*(1), 53–55.

Decker, L. E., & Decker, V. (2003). *Home, school, and community partnerships.* Lanham, MD: Scarecrow Press.

Delgado-Gaitan, C. (1994a). Consejos: The power of cultural narratives. *Anthropology & Education Quarterly, 25*(3), 298–316.

Delgado-Gaitan, C. (1994b). Socializing young children in Mexican-American families: An intergenerational perspective. In P. M. Greenfield & R. R. Cocking (Eds.), *Cross-cultural roots of minority child development* (pp. 55–87). Hillsdale, NJ: Lawrence Erlbaum.

Delgado-Gaitan, C. (2001). *The power of community: Mobilizing for family and community.* Boulder, CO: Rowman & Littlefield.

Elementary Secondary Education Act, Title I (ESEA) (The No Child Left Behind Act). (2001).

Epstein, J. L. (1987). Effects on student achievement of teachers' practices and parental involvement. In S. Silvern (Ed.), *Literacy through family community and school interactions* (pp. 98–110). Greenwich, CT: JAI Press.

Epstein J. L. (1994). Theory to practice: School and family partnerships lead to school improvement and student success. In C. L. Fagnango & B. Z. Werber (Eds.), *School, family, and community interaction: A view from the firing lines* (pp. 39–54). San Francisco: Westview.

Epstein, J. L. (2001). *School, family, and community partnerships: Preparing educators and improving schools.* Boulder, CO: Westview.

Finders, M., & Lewis, C. (1994). Why some parents don't come to school. *Educational Leadership, 51*(8), 50–55.

Flemming, L. (1982). *Parental influence on the educational and career decision of Hispanic youth.* Washington, DC: National Council of La Raza.

Fuller, M. L., & Olsen, G. (1998). *Home-school relations: Working successfully with parents and families.* Boston: Allyn & Bacon.

González, M. L. (1995, Spring). Like mother, like daughter: Intergenerational programs for Hispanic girls. *Educational Considerations, 22*(2), 17–30.

Haycok, K., & Duany, L. (1991, January). Developing the potential of Latino students. *Principal,* pp. 21–27.

Heller, C. (1966). *Mexican American youth: Forgotten youth at the crossroads.* New York: Random House.

Henderson, A. T., & Mapp, K. L. (2002). *A new wave of evidence: The impact of school, family, and community connections on student achievement.* Austin, TX: Southwest Educational Development Laboratory.

Henderson, R. W., & Garcia, A. B. (1973). The effects of parent training programs on the question-asking behavior of Mexican-American children. *American Educational Research Journal, 10*(3), 193–201.

Hispanic Policy Development Project. (1990). *Handbook for school personnel: "You're a Parent; You're a Teacher"* Washington, DC: Author.

Inger, M. (1993, April). Getting Hispanic parents involved. *Education Digest,* pp. 33–34.

Jayanthi, M., & Nelson, J. S. (2002). *Savvy decision making: An administrator's guide to using focus groups in schools.* Thousand Oaks, CA: Corwin Press.

Johnston, J. H., Markle, G. C., & Harshbarger, M. (1986, August). What research says about dropouts. *Middle School Journal, 17,* 8–17.

Jones, T. G. (2002). Incorporating Latino parents' perspective into teacher preparation. In *Research Digest Family Involvement Network* (The Harvard Family Research Project, Graduate School of Education). Cambridge, MA: Harvard University.

Jones, T. G., & Vélez, W. (1997, March 24–28). *Effects of Latino parent involvement on academic achievement.* Paper presented at the annual meeting of the American Educational Research Association, Chicago.

Laosa, L. M. (1983). School, occupation, culture, and family: The impact of parental schooling on the parent-child relationship. In I. E. Sigel & L. M. Laosa (Eds.), *Changing families* (pp. 79–136). New York: Plenum.

Lareau, A. (2000). *Home advantage: Social class and parental involvement in elementary education,* Boulder, CO: Rowman & Littlefield.

Lopez, G. R. (2002). The value of hard work: Lessons on parent involvement from an (im)migrant household. *Harvard Educational Review, 71*(3), 416–437.

Lucas, T., Henze, R., & Donato, R. (1990, August). Promoting the success of Latino language-minority students: An exploratory study of six high schools. *Harvard Educational Review, 60*(3), 315–340.

Moles, O. C. (1993). Collaboration between schools and disadvantaged parents: Obstacles and openings. In N. F. Chavkin (Ed.), *Families and schools in a pluralistic society* (pp. 71–98). New York: State University of New York Press.

National Center for Educatonal Statistics. (2002). *The condition of education* (Report 2002). Washington, DC: U.S. Department of Education.

Paige R., & Betka, S. (2001). Family involvement in children's education: Successful local approaches—An idea book. Washington, DC: U.S. Department of Education, Office of Educational Research and Improvement.

Reyes, P., Scribner, J. D., & Paredes-Scribner, A. (Eds.). (1999) *Lessons from high performing Hispanic schools: Creating learning communities.* New York: Teachers College Press.

Rodriguez, G. G. (1999). *Raising nuestros niños.* New York: Fireside Books.

Schecter, S. R., & Cummins, J. (Eds.). (2003). *Multilingual education in practice: Using diversity as a resource.* Portsmouth, NH: Heinemann.

Shannon, S. M. (1996). Minority parental involvement: A Mexican mother's experience and a teacher's interpretation. *Education & Urban Society, 29*(1), 71–84.

Sleeter, C. E. (2001). Preparing teachers for culturally diverse schools. *Journal of Teacher Education, 52*(2), 94–106.

Sosa, A. S. (1997 Spring-Summer). Involving Hispanic parents in educational activities through collaborative relationships. *Bilingual Research Journal, 21*(2&3), 1–8

Tomatzky, L., Cutler, R., & Lee, J. (1990a, August 28). College knowledge: What Latino parents need to know and why they don't know it. *El Paso Times,* p. B4.

Tomatzky, L., Cutler, R., & Lee, J. (1990b, August 28). Now that I've made it into mainstream I must not be Hispanic. *El Paso Times,* p. B4.

U.S. Bureau of the Census. (2000). *The foreign born population in the United States, 2000* (CPH-L98). Washington, DC: Author.

U.S. Department of Commerce. (n.d.). *Population projections of the United States by age, sex, race, and Hispanic origin: 1992 to 2050.* Washington, DC: Author.

U.S. Department of Education, Office of Educational Research and Improvement. (2001, June). *Family involvement in children's education: Successful local strategies.* Washington, DC: Author.

U.S. Department of Education. (2002, January 8). Online newsletter. Retrieved from www.ed.gov/nclb/landing.jhtml.

Velex-Ibañez, C. (1988). Networks of exchange among Mexicans in the U.S. and Mexico: Local level mediating responses to national and international transformation. *Urban Anthropology and Studies of Cultural Systems and World Economic Development, 17*(1), 27–51.

Index

Adolfo Perez, 2
Academic performance, 17, 32, 40, 94
Aspirations, 41, 64, 85, 91, 94, 131

Bilingual, 8, 17, 19, 24, 25, 27, 28, 32, 33, 36,
      48, 58, 63, 70, 72, 78, 79, 80, 99, 118,
      121, 122, 123

Chicanos, 2
Collaboration, 16, 76, 116, 123
Continuity, 3, 68, 70
Cuban, 1

Educación, 4,
Elementary, 3, 5, 6, 7, 9-11, 12, 15, 16, 17, 18,
      20, 21, 23, 24, 25, 26, 29, 30, 32, 33, 35,
      36, 37, 38, 39, 44, 46-52, 54, 56-58, 62-
      66, 70, 73-75, 77-79, 81-86, 88-89, 91, 94,
      96, 99, 100, 101, 105, 108, 109, 113, 116,
      124, 125, 129, 130
English-as-a-second language, 42, 134
English language learner, 18
English Language Development, 91
English literacy, 20
English proficiency, 56, 62
English speaker, 33, 79, 80, 117,
      119, 121, 123

Gabriel Garcia Marquez, 2

High school, 3, 18, 19, 26-27, 32,
      39-48, 51, 64, -655, 67, 71, 74, 77, 82, 83,
      85, 86, 88, 92, 94, 95, 96, 99, 101, 103,
      113, 123, 124, 125-126, 128, 129
Home activities, 41, 69, 70
Home culture, 31, 36, 73
Home-school connection, 6

Home visits, 31, 32, 37, 77, 107, 108, 109
Homework, 5, 7, 28, 30, 32, 35, 39, 41, 46, 47,
      48, 56, 57, 59, 60, 63, 67, 69, 72, 92, 94,
      100, 109, 117

Mario Molina, 2
Mexican, 1, 2, 55, 118, 120, 125
Mexican American, 1, 2, 134,
Middle school, 44, 46, 64, 68, 71, 86, 115, 128
Mother/Daughter Program, 82-88, 90,
      92, 94, 95
Multicultural, 98

Nontraditional activities, 19, 20, 89, 91
Networking, 113

OCO, 113-117
Octavio Paz, 2

Parent education, 8, 41, 57, 96,
      100, 103, 104, 116
Parent Resource Center, 103, 104, 105
Parent-teacher conferences, 33, 107
PICO, 113-115
Puerto Rican, 1, 2, 135

Resilience, 13, 42,
Respect, 3, 4, 7, 13, 21, 31, 36, 40, 48, 74, 114, 131
Rigoberta Menchu, 2

Sergio Robles, 2

Teacher preparation, 5, 81
Teacher preservice, 81
Traditional activities, 20
Trust, 16, 21, 40, 72, 80, 93, 94, 122
Tutors, 48, 72, 75, 84, 93, 123, 129

**CORWIN
PRESS**

The Corwin Press logo—a raven striding across an open book—represents the union of courage and learning. Corwin Press is committed to improving education for all learners by publishing books and other professional development resources for those serving the field of K-12 education. By providing practical, hands-on materials, Corwin Press continues to carry out the promise of its motto: **"Helping Educators Do Their Work Better."**